Giles AT WAR

Also by Peter Tory

Giles: A Life in Cartoons
The Giles Family

GILES AT WAR

PETER TORY

BCA

LONDON NEW YORK SYDNEY TORONTO

This edition published 1994
by BCA
by arrangement with
HEADLINE BOOK PUBLISHING

CN 3140

First published in 1994
by HEADLINE BOOK PUBLISHING

10 9 8 7 6 5 4 3 2 1

The photographs in this book have been supplied by courtesy of
Express Newspapers plc and Joan and Carl Giles,
with the exception of p. 91 (Lee Miller)

Design and computer page make-up by Penny Mills

Printed and bound in Great Britain by
BPC Hazell Books Ltd
A member of
The British Printing Company Ltd

For Alex, Ben and Kelly

Acknowledgements

I am most grateful to Chronicle Communications Ltd of
Farnborough, Hampshire, for their permission to use passages from
their book, *Chronicle of the Second World War*.

I would also like to thank Joan and Carl Giles as usual for their
endless help in preparing this book.

Finally, thanks, once again to Mark Burgess,
my tireless researcher in this project.

Contents

Giles AT WAR

Prologue

A group of figures in battledress crawled awkwardly along a shallow trench. As always in such situations, the principal fear was for the backside, that part of the anatomy which takes the highest position when its owner is on hands and knees. There was the rush of an artillery shell and an unpleasant bang. One of the group stopped briefly to wipe a piece of mud from the surface of his spectacles as a couple of crouching Tommies made way for the party to pass on down the trench.

As the chap in the glasses scrambled after his fellow soldiers, one of the pair of infantrymen turned to the other and said: ''Ere, do you know 'oo that is?'

''Oo?' enquired his chum.

'That was Giles.'

'What, you mean Giles?'

'Yes, mate, Giles. I saw him at HQ.'

'Blimey.'

It was, indeed, Giles. He was attached, at that point, to the Coldstream Guards, fulfilling his duties as a war correspondent for the *Daily Express* – not your ordinary

Giles poses with a gritty, soldier-like demeanour. He would have been quite happy to take up arms, but a motor-cycle injury in his youth left him mostly deaf in one ear. He also had poor sight. However, while concerned that cartooning was not the best way to go into battle, he was reassured wherever he went that his usually cheerful and sometimes powerful impressions of the conflict, at home and in Europe, gave enormous pleasure and encouragement to all who shared them.

He certainly entered into the spirit of combat. Giles rushed around in a jeep, carried a gun – a precaution not encouraged amongst correspondents – and pressed into areas of danger which had his Cockney driver, Reg Bishop, perspiring. The effect of spirit–raising humour and satire in such terrible times can never be measured – but Giles certainly did his bit for the war effort.

"The correct term, Private Wilson, when referring to a Commanding Officer is 'C.O.'. Not 'there goes the toffee-nosed old basket.'"

Daily Express, May 30th, 1943

Giles started drawing for the Daily *and* Sunday Express *in October 1943. Until then, all of his war-time cartoons appeared in the first national newspaper he worked for,* the left-wing Sunday journal, Reynolds News. *Here he introduces us to a selection of his favourite military types, from colonel to Tommy.*

correspondent, but a cartooning correspondent. There were a few of them at the front, but not many.

After another hundred yards Giles and his companions were confronted by a similar group of helmeted warriors, also on hands and knees, crawling in the opposite direction. There was no room to pass and both parties halted.

Giles peered at the grimy face beneath the helmet of the private leading the other group and saw startlingly familiar features. It took a moment or two to register, for you do not expect to meet anybody from your high street in a slit trench hundreds of miles from anywhere. Suddenly, there was recognition: the chap before him was his bank manager from Barclays, Ipswich.

'Well I'm blowed,' said the figure, whom Giles had last seen, the shafting light of summer afternoon illuminating his premature baldness, moving a soft and well-scrubbed index finger down the satisfactory black digits on the right-hand side of his bank account. 'You're Mr Giles. How are you?' The two rose into a hunched position in order to shake hands. An artillery shell whined over the position causing the pair to collapse onto their stomachs.

There was a further surprise to come.

'Here,' said the bank manager. 'I've got your brother-in-law in my lot. Come and say "Hello".' Thus, the two men, having sorted themselves out from the confusion, moved further down the trench in search of Carl's relative.

'He was in the khasi, in the shithouse,' recalls Giles. 'There we were all that way from home and he was in the trench shithouse. We had to hang around – me and my bank manager – listening to the horrible sound effects and waiting for him to finish.

'It's funny,' reflected Carl, 'but a bank manager is just the sort of bloke you'd expect to be in command of an untidy lot in the Home Guard. But there he was – in the thick of it.'

CHAPTER ONE

The Home Front

Giles knew all about the Home Guard. Now he was at war, sent into the heart of the conflict by his newspaper editor in order to dispatch cartoons to Fleet Street. But he had served for the first three years in the Home Guard. He had been a corporal, but had not really regarded himself as a fully fledged soldier. He was not a fellow to pull rank. But there were those, he recalls with amusement, who found that a uniform of any kind, topped with a helmet, gave them airs and graces which were quite preposterous.

On the Home Front, especially during the earlier years of the war, all kinds of people suddenly found themselves with giddy authority. For the first time in their lives, humble figures were able to stand before the bedroom mirror and proudly contemplate themselves in a uniform. Their new status came with a whistle and a notebook, and with the clearly vested power to demand attention and issue commands.

One such man Cyril Girling, resident grave-digger of Tuddenham, a small village just to the north of Ipswich. Cyril was a nice enough chap, but his role of digging six-feet deep, rectangular holes for the departed of that dozy corner of East Anglia hardly brought him into much social contact with the living. This was except – of course – for the regulars of The Fountain, Tuddenham's only tavern and the favourite over half a century of Carl Giles, Ipswich's most distinguished and most loved celebrity.

Giles's friends, far from being notables with grand jobs and titles, were largely drawn from the artisans of the community: builders, motor-car mechanics, farm labourers and sheep slaughterers. And, indeed, grave-diggers. Cyril was not only a fellow drinking mate of Giles in the smoke-swirling, eternally welcoming interior of The Fountain, but at his home down the road, Badger's Cottage.

One day Cyril Girling was summoned to the police station and told that he was to be Tuddenham's special constable. He was issued with a smart uniform, neatly pressed, and was given a pair of those big boots which made such a satisfyingly important sound when 'patrolling' the quiet streets and, especially, when stamping the feet for circulatory purposes beneath the lamp by Mrs Bywater's house just beyond the bridge.

Then came the day that Cyril Girling, known as 'Pockets', enjoyed his first visit – briefly attired in civvies – as special constable, to The Fountain. He drummed his fingers importantly on the bar when his pint was low, and simply nodded his head when the barman caught his eye. It was uncharacteristic, and Giles was amused by it. He never missed a trick when it came to observing the behaviour of the colourful characters of the tavern world.

"I let you drive—and what happens?...."

The notion of the private being cheeky to authority was of constant delight to Giles.

Some time later that evening, Giles was driving in his black Humber, headlights mere slits in accordance with blackout regulations, when he became aware of a figure just on the other side of Tuddenham Bridge stepping out of the shadows into the road. It was Cyril Girling in his new uniform, and he was waving his hand, palm downwards.

'The bugger was flagging us down,' recalls Giles.

Giles describes how, with a combination of curiosity and irritation, he stopped the car beside Cyril. The new special constable slowly unbuttoned his tunic pocket and removed his notebook and a pencil. He then licked the end of the pencil, observed it with deep satisfaction, and pushed his face close to Giles's.

" Come, Mr Brown. Let's hear you say in a loud clear voice: 'Move over to the right there, please!' "

It is curious that the business world of the capital bustled on in much the same way. As a Londoner, Giles knew the surreal, subterranean world of the tube like anyone else. The Underground system was used as a mass bomb shelter.

"We say to her: 'Friend or Foe?' and all she keeps saying is: 'Foe!'"

He didn't know it at the time, but acknowledged later, that the lady in this picture was one of the prototypes for his post-war tyrant and most famous Family character, Grandma.

'Name, sir, please,' he demanded.
Giles looked thunderstruck.
'Identification, please, sir,' ordered Cyril.
'But you know who I am, you silly sod,' yelled Giles.

'I'm sorry, sir, but it is my duty to ...'
'Bugger off,' shouted Giles. And with that he gunned his engine, squealed his back tyres with ferocious indignation and shot off into the war-time darkness.

"I'LL GIVE YOU 'OME GUARD!"

Giles was well aware of the inconvenience caused by the Home Guard – he was in it. He once arranged war games in north London, causing absolute bedlam. Smoke bombs polluted washing for a square mile of Edgware.

'You were really ruthless with him,' remembers Joan to this day.

'Silly sod,' repeated Giles, his fury unabated even half a century later.

What was significant about this village-street encounter was its illustration of the one thing that drove Giles – and still drives him – to distraction: the misuse of petty authority. His cartoons bristled with

21

"At a wild guess, Herr Gomm, I should say we are arriving at Whipsnade."

this dislike in every form over the years, settling finally in more recent times on that most hated of minor officials, the traffic warden.

Giles, who divided his time between London, a family home in his beloved East Anglia and finally a farmhouse outside Ipswich, was in the Home Guard, attached to the Middlesex Regiment. He was to have frequent encounters with those who should not have been in charge of a cement mixer, let alone a group of men whose job it was to defend the nation from the steel-helmeted hoards from over the Channel.

While living in his parents' semi in Edgware, the suburban dwelling upon which the cartoonist was to base the home of his famous post-war Family, Giles was particularly active in what became rather unfairly known – since it contained many young men – as Dad's Army.

He recalls: 'There was this funny little man called Lewis with glasses and what looked like a First World War joke moustache. He had no rank at all, but he loved dressing up in his uniform. Some of us thought he might sleep in it.

'Whoever you were you had a chance to lead the platoon. And Lewis couldn't wait for his turn. Off we would go, with Lewis shouting orders from the front as if he was changing the guard at Buckingham Palace. "Byyy the riiight," he would yell. "Quiiick maaarch." He would then march us all round Edgware. It took hours to get back, because he kept leading us the wrong way up streets and would get lost. Imagine being lost with a platoon in the middle of Edgware.

'He wouldn't admit he was lost, dismiss us and let us all find our way home for some tea. We just marched on and on, often passing the same row of shops three times in a period of half an hour. "Riiight turn," he would be shouting all importantly, and he wouldn't have the faintest idea where he was off to.'

The officers weren't much better. Giles, a private, frequently found himself attending emergencies of one kind or another. He would put on his helmet, grab his Lee Enfield .303 rifle and go charging down the street. With his specs and not entirely athletic demeanour Giles never cut the dash of an Errol Flynn, but he was a willing soul and one of the best shots in his unit.

One early morning in late summer Giles was awoken by an enormous thump and an explosion. The house had shaken and ornaments had lifted off the mantelpiece. Anyone who had heard the sound before recognised its particularly sickening significance: an aeroplane had crashed in the very near vicinity.

Giles scrambled into his uniform, tugged on his helmet, grabbed his rifle and sprinted down the street towards the pall of black oily smoke which was billowing up into the still morning air some eighty yards behind the house. Panting and perspiring, he arrived at a clearing by a housing estate to see the twisted, scattered wreckage of a British fighter, the fuselage of which was being reduced to white, glowing powder by a fierce petrol fire.

Giles jumped over a low wall and after getting as close as he could to the blaze and concluding that there was nothing he could do for anyone who might have been in the aircraft's cockpit, took up a position,

OPPOSITE: *Here is a glimpse of the dark side of Giles, which is otherwise not typical. His style often varied in his early days. A number of the Reynolds drawings are certainly not instantly recognisable as being from the hand of the master. Note the name Herr Gomm. Gomm was a Giles school mate.*

"What! You take orders from that funny little man in the corner with the big black whiskers?"

rifle at the ready, some fifty yards away. He stood guard for most of the day, keeping sightseers and ghouls at a distance, while being uncomfortably aware that his backside might be a target for any ammunition which had failed to explode in the wreck.

Indeed, he was surprised that it took so long for anyone of senior rank to turn up. Eventually his commanding officer, Captain Heatherington, jumped self-importantly over the same low wall and strode up to Giles with his swagger-stick tucked under his arm.

"And what's our little man found now?"

Apart from the terrifying act of the child, this is very unlike the Giles we know. The two parents seem to be from someone else's cartoon world altogether.

'All right, Giles,' he snapped, 'jolly good. I'll take over. Well done. Off you go.'

'Would you believe it?' asks Giles. 'Heatherington was mentioned in dispatches for his quick thinking and responsible action. Bloody cheek. No one mentioned me at all.'

Not all of the few incompetent and buffoon-like characters in the otherwise well-regarded Home

"I think I'm speaking for everyone, Grandpa, when I ask you to quit singing 'Run, Rabbit, Run!'"

Early Giles again.

Guard were to receive quite such a bad report from Private Giles. He remembers with affection and some compassion old Reg Hill, for example, not only the local sergeant but the diligent and kindly insurance man of Giles's future mother-in-law, Agnes Clarke.

It was Reg's duty to take his men on regular training exercises, most of which involved pack drill, running around, doing press-ups – and preparing for the worst. The obstacle course, however, was too much for him.

'We had to charge with full pack and rifle and quite literally run up this vertical wall,' recalls Giles. 'Reg was a wonderful insurance man, but this particular challenge was quite beyond him. He was supposed to show us the way, but every time he ran at the wall he just sort of crashed into it and fell down in a heap. Meanwhile, there were some old boys leaping over him and running up the thing like gazelles, vaulting over the top with the ease of

"All right, all right. You carry on. You'll soon find out WHY it's silly to sit there."

This was a recurring theme in Giles's war cartoons.

teenagers. Reg, our leader and inspiration, just kept on crashing and blundering about on the other side.

'I felt terribly sorry for him, but it was funny, really, when you saw people who normally wore suits and raised their hats to old ladies in the high street stumbling about with packs and rifles, with eyes popping and red faces. That was old Reg. He was much more at home in a suit sitting at a desk scratching away slowly and conscientiously with a pen.'

The time came when the talents of many of these various characters were to be stretched even further. The lads were to be required to combine their military

"At least he doesn't have a ———— sergeant bawling at him all day long."

It is the sergeant's monstrous look-alike child which catches the second glance of the eye here.

training with the thespian demands of showbusiness. The occasion was to be a major event: Display Day, a dramatic show of strength, firepower and efficiency for the benefit of the public. And Carl Giles, being the most artistic and creative figure in North London's home soldiery, was very much in charge. Captain

Heatherington had taken a shine to this bespectacled, rather amusing cartoonist with the quizzical expression; he saw Giles, with regard to the forthcoming show, as a kind of Cecil B. de Mille in khaki.

The idea was to stage, on the playing fields behind Whitchurch Lane, a noisy and fiercely fought rescue

"Perhaps our evacuee friends can enlighten us as to who placed Master Michael in the refrigerator last night."

Once again, Giles was amused by the idea of horrible little brats from the cities being foisted, as evacuees from the bombing, on the snooty occupants of grand country houses.

"Beef-eaters? We ain't beef-eaters. We live on Spam like everybody else."

Daily Express, Jan 10th, 1943

Spam was the tinned meat which almost everyone lived on during the war. It is described in today's dictionary as a loose, bland, unexciting luncheon meat made from pork, spices etc.

"He says he could hear a rattle or something."

operation. A number of women would be trussed and gagged by a group of Nazis and held captive in the huts at the far end of the field. The sheds, full of spiders and bits of old newspaper, were more usually the retreat for schoolmasters sheltering from the rain and for the initial medical care of boys with nose bleeds and ankle sprains suffered on the football field. The chaps of the Home Guard, shouting like merry hell, were to emerge from the side streets and sprint down Whitchurch Lane itself, vault the wall and run across

"For the last time, Madam, this is not the Baby Linen Counter."

Daily Express, Mar. 17th, 1940

Giles had not yet gone to war, but this and the following three cartoons offer the theme of the British serviceman prevailing with humour in all manner of circumstances.

the field, bayonets fixed and firing blank ammunition from their .303s. The women would be rescued and the Tommies would call the day their own. Triumph.

Giles, who had worked in the film world, threw himself into the arrangements with enormous gusto. Firstly and most importantly he had to hire the

"O.K. Sunshine. Drop your Ace on 'is Queen and 'op outside."

German uniforms. So the next day he called in on a theatrical costumiers. It was one of those dingy emporiums run by effete old men from another world which abounded even during the war round the backstreets of Soho and the West End.

'I would like a dozen German uniforms,' demanded Giles of a tall man in a cardigan and half glasses. 'Make them all average sort of size.'

The assistant, for whom the war was a particularly unpleasant business, looked distastefully over his specs for a long time at this figure in a casual leather jacket. Dame costumes, yes. A whole row of Widow Twankies, fittings for every size. Vikings, they could do without any bother, as they could Roman centurions and Eskimos. But Germans! And just like that, too. Without proper fittings.

UP IN THE CLOUDS

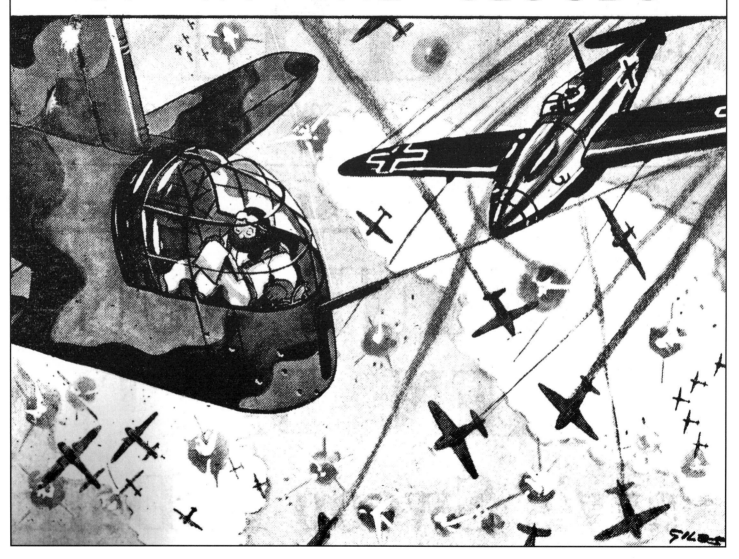

Dear Mum,
I'm sorry to hear Willie's got measles and that Uncle George fell down stairs but didn't hurt himself much . . . . .

". . . . And here's a pcture of my brother Fred when he was six!"

The assistant continued to look at Giles. Then, after some moments, he disappeared behind some togas and whispered with a colleague. There was the scraping sound of metal coat-hangers as a gap was created in the toga rack so that Giles could be studied by the other, as yet unseen, costumier. Germans, indeed.

'For how long will you be requiring them, sir?' Giles was asked, eventually, as two huge piles of bluish-grey *Wehrmacht* uniforms were thumped down on the counter.

'Till ve haf conquered the verld,' called Giles as he staggered out into the summer sunlight.

"I am afraid I must insist on da absolute quiet, please."

Sunday Express, Oct. 17th, 1943

The Germans caused devastation in Italy – they had flattened Naples and were looting Rome.

"Personally I think our dear Fuehrer is talking out of the back of his neck."

Daily Express, Nov. 25th, 1943

"Boy! They've just dropped a beaut! Smack in da jolly old Unter den Linden."

Daily Express, Nov. 30th, 1943

Lancaster bombers, supported by Mosquitos, had made their fourth major raid within a week on Berlin. How Giles's 'Musso' loved to torment the Führer.

Little was to go smoothly in this great showbusiness endeavour. Giles's mother was approached, and asked whether she would mind being one of the bound and gagged women. 'Bugger off,' she said. Giles's father, a busy man with two successful tobacconists to run, was equally unenthusiastic. He was asked if he could be one of the 'peasants', an extra who would be required to stand around and look frightened.

"This is the last time I do this ruddy trip without a convoy."

Sunday Express, Dec. 26th, 1950

Santa Claus, even in the post-war suburbia of southern England, never got a particularly gentle ride from Giles's pen. Still, this is a pretty grim Christmas cartoon.

"I'd like to see <u>them</u> ven they 'af been out here a veek or two."

Daily Express, Jan. 23rd, 1944

"These damn Japs are showing us all up—we shall have to think up a few new ones."

Daily Express, Feb. 3rd, 1944

Giles would occasionally abandon his comical representation of the war's protagonists, with devastating effect. This is as close to sheer horror as Giles's cartoon work ever came.

"Ain't there enough trouble in the world without you coming in here saying you've got measles?"
(It is alleged that Mussolini is probably ill)

Sunday Express, Feb. 13th, 1944

"Come out of the road—you'll get run over."

Sunday Express, Mar. 5th, 1944

Low-level flying in Holland, probably en route to Germany. Such flying was known as hedge-hopping. In Bomber Command the air crews' chance of survival was estimated at fifty/fifty.

"Can I help you, boys?"

Daily Express, April 4th, 1944

Hitler's self-appointed jester gives his master an unwelcome reminder of Napoleon.

A quiet and reserved man, he came close to showing strong emotion on this occasion. 'Bugger off,' he said, too.

In the event it was Giles's pretty wife Joan and Giles's sister Eileen who were persuaded to play the parts of the women. Giles even painted huge boards to look like ruined walls of buildings, complete with shell holes, and stood them about the perimeter of the intended action.

'In the end everything went wrong,' remembers Giles. 'The walls fell over, there was complete confusion. The worst thing of all was that the smoke from the smoke bombs, with there being no wind, just hung about and slowly drifted into people's houses. Washing was ruined and the smell was dreadful. People were very angry.'

The action itself was farcical. And very dangerous.

'Imagine,' says Giles. 'There were all these blokes running into thick smoke with fixed bayonets, firing blanks and shouting like merry hell – it's a wonder that no one was killed. Fortunately they all missed one another in the fog and ran out at opposite ends. If it had been a real battle it might have been the end of the war.'

And where was the fearless Captain Heatherington during all this?

'Oh, he knew it was going to be a cock-up,' recalls Giles. 'He stood at a safe distance, looking at his watch and pretending not to be involved. He wasn't going to lower himself by being part of that kind of nonsense.'

In the Home Guard wearing a uniform and chasing about with a rifle was, in a sense, a bit of a lark. The same could not be said for others. Scattered across the face of the planet, in jungles and muddy ditches, on beaches and in bomb craters, in the clanging hulls of submarines and in the bowels and on the bridges of ships, in the tail turrets of Lancaster bombers and in the blister hangars of the desert, were ordinary Britons for whom a uniform had always been something you wore for the annual Christmas play in the village hall or school gymnasium.

They were butchers and bakers and bankers and car-dealers, sweeps and sheep slaughterers, boiler-makers and bell-ringers, clerks and clippies, union men and undertakers, oyster fishermen and overseers, boffins and blackguards, tinkers, tailors and toffs.

Carl believed, for all his patriotism and brave willingness to join his brothers-in-arms in combat, that he would have to make do with his efforts on the Home Front. He wasn't to know that before long he would be in the thick of the bloody European Theatre, witnessing things which turned him from an innocent and callow young artist into a cynical and hardened veteran.

Meanwhile, for the time being, Giles was restricted on medical grounds to protecting Blighty.

Even Joan was pressed unwittingly into service for the Home Guard, and she came to the rescue more than once, too. On one occasion, Giles found himself summoned to headquarters with little warning and without being given time to return home for his rifle.

Joan, with misgivings but with her husband's reputation and dedication to duty foremost in her mind, took the weapon from its cupboard. Carrying it awkwardly in both hands, she walked a considerable distance to join the queue at the local bus-stop. Fellow travellers looked at her with a mixture of alarm and curiosity. Those on the top floor of the bus carrying Joan and the lethal weapon to the barracks some three miles away felt it wise not to challenge her or to sit in the immediate vicinity.

'It was probably loaded,' says Joan. 'It always amuses me to think of that, because you have to imagine what would happen if a young woman took a gun on a bus today. She would probably be shot from the top of a building by the SAS. But it was war, and I suppose people just sort of accepted it.'

Joan, in any case, was a sturdy soul. And Giles had no greater ally, then or later. It was not generally known that Giles and Joan, who had no children, were first cousins. They grew up together and never entertained the slightest notion that one day they would be man and wife. When it suddenly dawned on Giles that he was in love with the kid who had now grown to be a young woman, he recalls: 'She was the prettiest girl I had ever seen.'

Joan also proved to be strong, endlessly patient – and goodness, she had to be patient – practical, charming and courageous. In the war she was so much a recognisable English product of the thirties and forties. We have all seen her type in black and white movies: the serene heroine who can be imagined standing on a dockside or a station platform as the troops go off to Southampton. She is the one, the steam of the locomotive swirling about her, who slowly raises her hand in farewell and doesn't weep.

With Giles in the Home Guard it seemed inconceivable that she would ever have to see her husband go off to war.

Giles, as a lad in short trousers, found nothing more fascinating than peering through the railings of a military barracks. He was mesmerised by soldiery, a fact reflected in the skill and detail which he brought to his drawing of military subjects. Study the rifles, study the uniforms – British, American, Japanese, French, German or Russian – and you will see that everything is as it should be, every button, bolt and brass buckle.

Historians and scholars would do worse than to study the war-time work of Giles as a record of pinpoint accuracy in matters of equipment. Even his vehicles show every nut and bolt, every spare tyre of the exact type and mark which would have been issued by the various stores, from Tokyo to Aldershot.

His studies began when he could scarcely walk. On Sundays, when the family lived in Islington, Giles would be taken by his father to Wellington Barracks, adjacent to Buckingham Palace. There he would watch the rehearsals for great ceremonial performances such as the Changing of the Guard. Mesmerised by the spectacle, he would note not merely the detail of the belts and bearskins, but the famous ramrod spine of the regimental sergeant major, the cut of his shoulders, the small spiky moustache and the sudden appearance of a massive set of white teeth each time he opened his mouth as wide as a howitzer barrel to bellow, bark or screech – often in window-shattering falsetto – an order to his five-acre parade-ground of men.

Giles's earliest memory of being stirred to the bottom of his being by the sound and sight of military spectacle concerned a man described exactly as above: Uncle Arthur, the man who married his mother's sister. Arthur served in the First World War as a sergeant major with the Coldstream Guards, and was, remembers Giles, a figure of ferocious honour and decency. And discipline.

'I remember I got hold of an air rifle – it could do quite a lot of damage. My uncle confiscated it, took the spring out of it and gave it back to me. I was very angry, but I didn't dare say anything. I was too terrified.'

Such fierce acts of adult common sense apart, Uncle Arthur stood tall and magnificent to the tiny Giles, an incomparable personal hero.

'I used to spend so much time up in Norwich at

"Don't let that fool you—it doesn't include their army."

Daily Express, April 27th, 1944

D-Day approaches: it is six weeks away.

my grandmother's house,' recalls the cartoonist, 'that we went to school up there. After classes I would go and stand with my little friends at the huge gates of Mousehold Heath Barracks, where my uncle was stationed. We usually didn't see him, just a lot of figures marching up and down in the distance. Then one day he appeared. It was the most exciting moment of my childhood.

'There was this frightening clattering noise from inside the barracks, and suddenly these four powerful, shining black horses with great leather harnesses thundered into view, towing a line of gun carriages.

'They broke into a canter as they went through the gate and then out onto the cobblestones. You have never heard such a bloody noise.

'And there, sitting up high beside the chap with the reins, was my uncle. He was straight and proud, with the peak of his cap over his eyes and his arms folded. He didn't glance to the right or to the left – just in front of him. He looked like a soldier should look. It was a fine sight.

'You can imagine the pride you'd feel. I turned to my chums and said: "That's my uncle."'

Uncle Arthur, when he retired, went into service, first with the Bishop of Norwich, then with the celebrated equestrian artist, A.J.Munnings, a wealthy man who lived in considerable style in Suffolk.

'My uncle made the perfect butler, and my aunt was the housekeeper. She was a small, dear lady – a funny, frightened little woman. They were a wonderful couple.'

Giles, in all respects, enjoyed an enchanted childhood. He was born during the Great War on 29 September, 1916, next to a pub at the Angel, Islington. The raucous merriment which rose up from below and penetrated his cot was to have a profound effect on the young mite's life. He spent his adult existence in taverns; there was scarcely a pub in Fleet Street, in Ipswich, or on the banks of the various Suffolk waterways which had not enjoyed the lavish and often noisy patronage of Giles and his occasionally musical band of merry-makers.

As Giles came into the world, offering to those who peered curiously into his bundle of swaddling garments a button-nosed, startled little figure very much like every drawing of an infant which ever appeared in a Giles cartoon, war raged across Europe.

On the Somme a new weapon, conceived and built in secrecy and known under the code name 'Tank', had temporarily put the terrified Germans to flight. 'These motor monsters,' it was reported in the newspaper that dropped onto the doormat in the Giles home, 'have transformed the whole character of the war and prisoners are saying: "Now Germany is kaput."' It was not the case, and that dreadful conflict was to continue for another two years.

Not many miles from the Giles house, at the time of the much-celebrated birth, an Essex constable had been awakened in the early hours by the sinister humming of a German Zeppelin. While he was frantically pulling on his clothes the droning ceased. Moments later there was the 'whoomph' of a huge though curiously woolly and soft-sounding explosion.

The constable raced from his house, still buttoning his tunic, and ran towards the bright flames which illuminated the base of the low cloud. He met a group of Germans, the Zeppelin's crew, walking towards him. The officer stopped, adjusted the strap under his helmet, and placed the whole lot under arrest. A military escort was summoned by much blowing of a whistle, and the prisoners were marched into custody.

Despite the effect of what was undoubtedly the most exciting incident in his career, an act of initiative and constabulary bravery reported in all the nation's newspapers, the policeman was back by the afternoon directing traffic in his home town of Cockfosters.

The drama, of course, had all the ingredients of a Giles cartoon.

Giles's young life was little affected by the savagery over the Channel. He had few relatives involved in the fighting, and lived in a home, unlike most infants, where there was no regular sight of an adult in a uniform. His father, a decent, quiet man, was a

"Station, Herr Major? This is the station."

Sunday Express, April 30th, 1944

tobacconist with successful though modest businesses in Islington and the Barbican. The Giles homestead was a happy place, blessed six years later by the arrival of sister Eileen, a lass much loved by her brother but a victim, nevertheless, of almost endless mischief. Readers of an earlier volume may recall that Giles's favourite game was to wind his sister's dolls, teddy bears and paint tubes through their mother's mangle.

Another misery endured by the long-suffering Eileen was the regular ordeal of being placed high on a scarlet pillar box and left, a mute prisoner on a tower, while her brother played in the streets, untroubled by tiresome female attentions, with his friends.

If all this suggests an aggressive, even warlike nature, it would be misleading. Giles, who was soon to attend Barnsbury Park School in Islington, quickly developed into an impressively creative lad. He played the violin and, more significantly, showed a brilliant talent for elegantly drawn graffiti and astonishingly accurate caricatures of pupils and staff – particularly the now notorious schoolmaster, Chalkie – in his exercise books.

It was Giles's natural, entirely untutored talent as an artist which was to earn him early teenage employment as an animator in the cartoon studios of Sir Alexander Korda. His experience on film, it can be seen from his subsequent cartoon drawing, gave his 'still' work an incredible feeling of movement, of a scene merely being a frame in a sequence, with a life before and after and beyond. This is particularly so in much of his war work.

It was during the period with Alexander Korda that Giles was involved in a nearly catastrophic motor-cycle crash, an accident which left him deaf in one ear and ineligible, come 1939, for conventional military service.

The Korda offices had moved from Elstree to Isleworth. At about that time, Giles, who was to have a long and expensive romance with fast and glamorous machinery, had purchased a Panther 600 motorbike. It was kicked into action with a violent thrust of the right heel, and Giles, suddenly a fierce figure, wore large gauntlets and goggles to ride it. All God's creatures scattered at his coming.

Giles rounded a corner at high speed on his way to work one morning in 1933, and hurtled straight into the grille of a large lorry which was passing the studio gates.

He remembers nothing. But he was incapacitated for nearly a year. He had fractured his skull and, almost as seriously, done grave damage to his drawing hand, and in particular to his thumb.

It was his first cousin, Joan, who regularly visited him in hospital, though neither can recall whether it was romance or duty which brought the attractive teenager to the Giles bedside. Indeed, the curious thing about the lifetime partnership which was eventually to follow is that there seems to be no recollection of when the close family friendship of youth changed to dalliance. Whatever the truth, the lives of the two cousins were to remain intertwined, by both design and accident, until they were finally blessed in union at the altar.

CHAPTER TWO

The Blitz

War approached. Both Joan and Giles found themselves working in newspapers, Joan as a secretary with the *News Chronicle* and Giles, in his first job as a full-time cartoonist, at *Reynolds News*, the left-wing Sunday paper owned by the Co-op and situated at the top of Gray's Inn Road near King's Cross.

An agreeable image of the young Giles at work is recalled by his former colleague, crusading left-wing journalist, Gordon Schaffer, now in his eighties. 'Giles,' says Gordon, 'had an easel in the library. And goodness, how he enjoyed working on his cartoons. He would do a bit – draw a character – then stand back and say, with a huge grin on his face: "Look at that silly bugger there." We didn't know how famous he was going to be.'

There were good days, says Giles. Marvellous days. The young cartoonist, whose work was rapidly gaining a large following, was quickly befriended by the writers on *Reynolds*, a number of them leading Communist commentators of the day. They included Alan Hutt and Monty Slater, the former a celebrated columnist and expert on printing, the latter also a columnist and a noted librettist. Slater produced the words for Benjamin Britten's celebrated opera, *Peter Grimes*. These were men of intellect, culture, enlightenment and charm. To Giles they became heroes.

The Spanish Civil War was at its height then, and the Communist struggle against Fascist Franco was drawing many young idealists from Europe and America into the conflict. Countless poets and artists were involved, hundreds giving their lives. Giles was deeply impressed.

Interestingly, one description of him by a Fleet Street editor very much fitted the image of those youngsters who went to Spain to fight, scarcely trained, in the International Brigade. 'Giles,' he wrote, 'is slight, his fair hair is extremely untidy, he peers at you with a quizzical, puckered face, and he usually wears a pair of wide, uncreased baggy trousers and often a leather golfing jacket.'

Giles didn't go off to fight. But his Communist sympathies, more emotional than practical, have remained with him – curiously, in some respects – through a life of great good fortune and prosperity. It has been tempting, on occasions, to challenge him on his politics, though there is no need. They prove not to be complicated: Giles has compassion, and the overwhelming complexities of ideologies leave him baffled.

Meanwhile, the ideologies of the Fascist leaders of Europe, Hitler and Mussolini, already emerging as

"What a beautiful morning! It wouldn't surprise me if you get your invasion this morning."

Daily Express, May 4th, 1944

leading comic characters in the cartoons of Giles, had been creating the ever darker certainty of another terrible conflict. While Mussolini had, for the time being, pledged to stay out of the scrap, Hitler was now hell-bent on lighting the fuse.

On 31 August, 1939, a month before Giles's twenty-third birthday, the words from Berlin agencies tickertaping into the *Reynolds News* office, and into every other newspaper around the world, left little doubt. A typical report was offered under the

"One more crack out of you about Kentucky Minstrels and someone's going
to start an invasion right here."

Sunday Express, May 7th, 1944

"There 'e goes—says he's going to get this ruddy invasion over, then get some leave."

Sunday Express, May 14th, 1944

D-Day is now three weeks away. This is a good example of the detail of both the hardware and the uniforms. Giles was accurate in such things down to the last rivet and button. Elsewhere in this collection it is worth comparing the equipment of the various armies which he also observed meticulously.

headline 'Countdown to War; Hitler Moves Against Poland': Dateline, Berlin, 31 Aug.

The world will soon be at war. After months of threats Hitler is within hours of launching his tanks and dive bombers against Poland.

The spark was lit tonight when the body of a murdered concentration camp inmate dressed in Polish army uniform was dumped at the German radio station at Gleiwitz on the Polish border, a few shots fired and a proclamation broadcast in Polish.

Few people believe this hoax, but it is good enough to provide the Germans with the pretext to start the fight for which Hitler has been spoiling ever since he was denied his war against Czechoslovakia when Britain and France surrendered to his demands at Munich.

After he had gobbled up Czechoslovakia it was obvious Poland was the next on his list and Neville Chamberlain, the British Prime Minister, decided that he had to be stopped. On 31 August, speaking for Britain and France, he promised Poland 'all support in their power'.

German tanks clattered and squeaked over the Polish border at dawn on 1 September. At 11.15 on 3 September, a sunny Sunday morning in London, Chamberlain broadcast a message to the nation advising it that Herr Hitler had not shown any intention of withdrawing from Poland and 'consequently this country is at war with Germany'.

Giles and Joan, with Joan's mother, had been listening to their wireless at the family home in Great Percy Street. Giles had stayed the night with his cousin. He often did. Great Percy Street was within walking distance of *Reynolds News* and anyway, as Giles says to this day, there was no impropriety in spending the night under the same roof as your cousin, kissin' or otherwise.

Giles's reaction to Chamberlain's broadcast on that golden late summer morning has caused, and continues to cause, the most astonishing, wonderfully silly argument about how he conveyed the tidings to his parents. The dispute serves to illustrate the nature of the argy-bargies which have always been a feature of the couple's never dull nor serene relationship.

Giles's mother and father lived in Edgware. They were not on the telephone, and may well have failed to hear the announcement of war. In any case, the event caused a tremendous amount of excitement for the young cartoonist, who felt it was his duty to bear this shattering news with the greatest urgency.

'I ran all the way to Edgware,' recalls a proud Giles as he sits in his wheelchair by the open French windows of his Suffolk farmhouse.

'What utter nonsense,' complains Joan, suddenly stopping with her tea-towel at the kitchen door. 'It's ten miles.'

'I tell you I ran,' shouts Giles over his shoulder. 'And it's not ten miles. What do you know?'

'You drove, Carl,' says Joan, reappearing and waving the towel with frustration. 'You had a small sports car. You drove.'

'What would you know about it, woman,' he yells with increasing grumpiness. 'Bloody women.'

Joan pops her head round the kitchen door. 'Because I was there.'

'She doesn't know anything. Why do women always get it wrong?'

A little later, in the kitchen, Joan says quietly: 'He drove.'

'What was that, woman?' thunders Giles from the French windows, his hearing suddenly showing both remarkable range and accuracy.

It is not right for the author of this volume to take

"The English say they never cast any clouts until May is out. O.K.—so we don't get any invasion this month."

Sunday Express, May 21st, 1944

"It's all right, son—we're only looking at you. Just so's we remember what you're like."

Daily Express, May 25th, 1944

Two weeks to go.

sides in these differences. However, there is one thing that is just a little puzzling and which adds more than a little weight to Joan Giles's view on this matter. Giles likes to tell the story of how he was daily tormented by children tampering in the street outside the office with his sports car.

"Watch this, Bert—this is going to be funny."

Sunday Express, June 4th, 1944

Giles, in gruesome frame of mind, is temporarily distracted from D-Day by forthcoming events in Rome.

"Himmel! Tourists!"

Sunday Express, June 11th, 1944

D-Day plus five.

"Control yourself, Hermann! What would Churchill say if he saw you."

Daily Express, June 14th, 1944

D-Day blues.

'I always had open cars,' he says, 'and whenever I looked down I would see a kid sitting in it at the wheel. I would go racin' down the stairs and usually couldn't catch 'em.

'Once I did, and I grabbed the little bugger and dragged him into *Reynolds News*. I had intended to give him a clip round the ear he would remember for the rest of his horrible life, but he made so much noise that I just let him go.

'I discovered later I had frightened him so much that he peed in my car.'

There is little purpose in this story except to illustrate – apart from Giles's notoriously fierce way with small children – that while he was at *Reynolds* he had a motor car which was constantly in use. It was efficient and well maintained. Why, then, would he have run all the way from Great Percy Street to Edgware in order to tell his mother that war had been declared? Had the vehicle broken down? Was it in the garage? Who will ever know?

Whatever the truth of it, there is something agreeably romantic about the notion of the young Carl Giles, fleet of foot like some runner in an earlier war, sprinting across plain and through mountain pass, bearing burning news of catastrophe to his beloved mother. That, as far as this book is concerned, shall be the official version.

So, war came once again to Europe. And to London. And to Gray's Inn Road. Suddenly, and absurdly, journalists – of the Home Guard variety – were seen going to work at *Reynolds News* with weapons. Executives appeared as corporals and young reporters as captains. Air raid sirens blared, leaving hacks far too concerned with their scoops working at their typewriters. From Giles's colourful recollections, and from his glorious war-time cartoons, we see the comical manner in which life, even in the darkest

times, presented itself to his ever-vigilant eye.

'I was working on a cartoon at ten o'clock one evening when there was one hell of a bang. A bomb of some kind had crashed into the top floor where all the printing equipment was. We assumed it hadn't gone off.

'So what does everyone do? They all troop upstairs to have a look at it. That's what people do with bombs. Amazin', isn't it? They go and look at them.'

There was another comical incident which could, like many funny things in war-time, have caused injury and death.

Explained Giles: 'A lot of the Home Guard journalists had their guns propped up against the wall or filing cabinets. They would even go off to the pub with them at lunchtime.

'You can imagine the scene in the office: a long room with lines of desks; the editor's office at the end, and all these newspaper chaps with uniforms and guns.

'One day an officer came in and one of the blokes stood up, snapped his heels together and banged his machine gun on the floor. He had left his safety catch off and – you can imagine the terrifying noise in that confined space – put six rapid shots through the ceiling.

'I've never seen men move so fast in my life; they were under the desks, behind the lockers, down the stairs as fast as they could move. I had disappeared as quickly as any of 'em. Down to the pub, I think. Any excuse...! And that was one of the best excuses I can remember. With machine guns going off in the newsroom even cartoons can wait.'

Pubs! Getting pissed! Newspapermen have never changed. Nor have the taverns which serve them, although Fleet Street, as the profession's premier village, is itself no more, entirely taken over by advertising men and lawyers. Still, older warriors will

"Didn't the B.B.C. say that he went back on TUESDAY!"

Daily Express, June 16th, 1944

Churchill had visited the Normandy beaches in the company of General Montgomery.

"It's ridiculous to say these flying bombs have affected people in ANY way."

Daily Express, July 11th, 1944

Germany's new weapon, the V1 flying bomb, was an all-metal monoplane powered by a ramjet engine and capable of 400mph. When it had reached its required distance, the engine cut out and it glided silently to earth, exploding with huge force. Londoners were severely spooked by the menace.

Giles drew this gloomy study of Arnold Russell, his news editor at Reynolds News, *doing sentry duty for the* Home Guard *in a Richmond graveyard. Giles didn't like the fellow much.*

probably enjoy recalling the war-time days in the King's Head and the Pindar of Wakefield, both public houses of much merriment which have welcomed generations of journalists. The former was near the old *Daily Worker* headquarters in King's Street, a minute's stroll from *Reynolds*, and the latter, a rather grander establishment, was in Gray's Inn Road itself.

It was to the Pindar or the King's Head that Giles would regularly repair either at what was known as opening time or at any other time when an opportunity presented itself. The cartoonist would stand, his legs slightly apart, jingling the money in his pocket with one hand and closely nursing his glass and cigarette in the other, while his specs reflected the smoky yellow light and the flickering and flashing noisy bustle. Giles was, essentially, a gregarious soul who adored good company, and who always held his own, whether it be with incoherent drunks or with the most sophisticated and clear-headed of fellow imbibers.

Assembled about him here, in this particular pub world just down the road from King's Cross, would be his Communist mates: Alan Hutt, notable for his beret; Monty Slater, with his huge enveloping raincoat; Gordon Schaffer with his views; and, always to Giles's distaste, the journal's news editor, Arnold Russell.

Giles to this day retains a ferociously unfriendly recollection of the man. He observes, shifting his weight in his wheelchair: 'I hated the sight of him. He was a typical Tory fart, typifying the little capitalist shit that Alan Hutt and Gordon and Monty would warn us all about. He was difficult as a news editor, too. Bad tempered, always firing off at everything.

'We all knew him as the terror of Richmond Gulch. In his first week in the Home Guard he had been posted to a lonely vigil as a sentry in Richmond Graveyard. I did a cartoon of him looking as miserable as sin surrounded by tombstones.'

Why, some might wonder, should Giles carry such an obsessively unfriendly memory of this uncharismatic man? There would seem, on examination, to be a very good reason, and we will return briefly to the subject in a few pages.

Each evening the pub door would open briefly, and into the scarcely breathable interior would slip a girl in her early twenties whom Giles had described as 'the prettiest girl I ever met in my life'. It was, of course, Joan Clarke, Giles's first cousin and a relatively humble employee in the newsroom of the *News Chronicle*. Every day after work – except on Sunday when she was required to do the late evening shift – she would put on her coat, adjust her hair, add a dab of lipstick and make her way on foot up to the excitement of the Pindar of Wakefield or the King's Head.

The presence of German bombers high above never seemed to make much difference, either to Joan's journey or to the enthusiasm of the revelries at her destination. For example, Giles recalls that the Pindar twice lost most of its glass – while the place was full.

Joan describes how she would duck and dive her way north up Gray's Inn Road during a raid, stopping here and there to peer out and observe the distant fire and smoke, or the bright, thin slats of the searchlights independently sweeping the malevolent heavens above the capital.

How strange it seems, to those of us who are too young, to consider the astonishing fact that people 'went out in it' as if it were merely heavy rain; drank in pubs and attended restaurants and theatres; and, in the case of Giles and his newspaper colleagues, worked on through the terror and the madness to ensure that their endeavours made the news stands in the dusty, slow-smoking ruins of dawn.

"Roll up your map, Herr General—I don't think your counter-attaqck's going to come off.

Sunday Express, July 16th, 1944

This was one of the rather infrequent appearances in a Giles cartoon of General Montgomery.

"I hope you won't think me unduly inquisitive, Benito, but just where were you on Thursday afternoon?"

Sunday Express, July 23rd, 1944

On 20 July, 1944, Count Claus von Stauffenberg, a courageous member of a conspiracy to kill Hitler, left a briefcase bomb in the conference room at the dictator's 'Wolf's Lair' headquarters near Rastenberg, East Prussia. The Führer was studying a map with a magnifying glass when the device exploded, but was saved from serious injury by the position of the bomb under the table. Hitler's eardrums were punctured, his right arm was temporarily paralysed and his legs were burnt. Had Stauffenberg been successful he would undoubtedly have changed history, possibly bringing the war to an early end.

"Now I want you to promise me you're all going to be really good little evacuees and not worry his Lordship."

Sunday Express, July 30th, 1944

The new terror of the flying bomb blitz on London brought a second evacuation of its younger citizens.

Come thousand-pound bomb or incendiary, Joan would make her way through the Blitz to be at the side of the man she had known since she was in a cot, who as a child cousin she had idolised, who as a teenager she had adored and found amusing. And who, as a twenty-six-year-old, a brilliant cartoonist increasingly acclaimed not just by her but by the world, she loved as a romantic partner.

'Romantic partner,' scoffs Giles with transparent mischief, in his wheelchair. He calls out, 'In the Blitz, were we romantic partners?' There is silence. Joan is outside. 'Where is that bloody woman,' growls Giles. Joan returns. 'Yes, Carl, what do you want?'

'Were we romantic partners in the Blitz?' Joan laughs. 'Well, I think we were by then.' Giles considers this for a moment. 'Well, I know you drank like a bloody fish.' Like a fish? It is obviously a silly accusation. Joan has never done anything to excess. Joan laughs again with a small shake of the head and goes about the routine which daily supports – has always supported in health and sickness – her beloved husband.

Whatever is said now, there was little doubt to the observers of the day that Carl Giles and Joan Clarke were very much in love. Indeed, they were shortly to be married, though their touching and enduring partnership was very nearly to be cut short in horrific circumstances.

Giles and Joan worked and lived in one of the most dangerous areas of London, outside of the docks. Joan's home in Great Percy Street, where Giles frequently spent the night, was only a few hundred yards away from the offices of *Reynolds News*. The two addresses were in the almost direct line formed by London's principal railway stations – Liverpool Street, Euston, King's Cross and St Pancras, Marylebone and Paddington. Each of these was a primary target for the Luftwaffe.

It was spring, 1941. The bombardment of British cities was at its height. A report on 21 March read:

London and the South East have been the main target in the Luftwaffe's spring night raids. One 500-pound bomb hit a crowded suburban dance hall. Of 150 dancers – munition workers, soldiers on leave and girl typists in party frocks – four, including three girls, were killed. It was disclosed yesterday that the Germans made a deliberate attempt to destroy Buckingham Palace last week. The attack began with the dropping of flares, which lit up the Palace; showers of incendiary bombs followed. The Germans then began to make low-level bombing runs. The palace escaped a direct hit.

The attacks on London, by this time, had become brutal and relentless. Over the Channel, Luftwaffe aircrews, briefed by their commanders before huge wall charts of the British capital, were becoming as familiar with the layout of London as Londoners themselves.

On the night of 16 April, Giles was working at his desk as the first wave of German bombers picked out the great S-bend in the Thames, east of the City, and began their run – via the docks – over the centre of London. Five hundred aircraft were to drop 100,000 bombs on the capital that night, in one of the worst bombing raids of the war. The fires of the incendiaries spread a glow about the capital, a glow which appeared from above to come from within the earth itself, illuminating the dome of St Paul's Cathedral and the huge vaulting roofs, further west, of the railway stations.

Near King's Cross, the bespectacled Giles, utterly preoccupied as ever with his work, and refusing – as did his colleagues – to take any form of cover, bent

"What's cooking, Honey?"

Daily Express, Aug. 1st, 1944

The Allies were pushing ahead.

"Having the time of your lives this time last year, weren't you?"

Daily Express, Aug. 10th, 1944

over his sketch. A few hundred yards away down Great Percy Street, Joan, by now Giles's fiancée, was attempting to sleep on the ground floor of the house. In the basement flat, sheltering under a table, were Joan's mother, Agnes, and three of her aunts. The bombs were shaking the foundations. Agnes eventually called upstairs and persuaded Joan to take proper refuge.

All of this had become very much a routine in this household, as in the other houses down this normally

"Them and their Second Fronts—gone and messed up our chances of an invasion over 'ere, that's what they've done."

Sunday Express, Feb. 12th, 1950

Those members of the Home Guard who wished to see action were accepting that the chances of a marauding German army on British soil were becoming regrettably remote.

quiet Victorian street. People either tried to sleep and ignore the bombing in their accustomed places of slumber, snoozed fitfully in cupboards and under protective lintels, or huddled together beneath tables – specially fortified or not – often in the basement. The Clarke family were little different. They favoured a table in the cellar. They would play cards on it when the hellish thunder sounded at a fairly safe distance, and crawled under it for shelter when the din drew near.

Being the Clarke/Giles family, they took a fairly spirited view of this rather unorthodox form of late-night socialising, and even gambled modestly on their card games.

Giles would often join them when he wasn't working; there they would be, the young cartoonist and the woman in his life, giggling and laughing as Hitler's grim-faced airmen, their features illuminated by the burning city below, tried to blow them to bits.

Recalls Giles: 'I can remember Joan's mother – a marvellous little woman and very, very funny – sitting under the table when the bombs got a bit close, and keeping her hand up on the surface so that she could protect her little pile of money from any rival hand which might shift a bit of it round the table-top.'

Giles uses the word 'little' as a term of endearment. A little woman or a little pile of money were both regarded by the artist as things to love and to be amused by. 'Little', to Giles, gives a subject an innocence, a safeness and an acceptability. The description of the little woman with her little pile of money creates in two deft brushstrokes a vivid picture. Giles perceived the world in cartoons. Even he would have been hard-pushed, however, to have been very amused by what happened next.

The bombers had started to make their runs, roughly east to west, down the line of the principal railway stations. This was only just north of the line formed by *Reynolds News* and the Clarke home in Great Percy Street. From the belly of one of the Heinkel One-Elevens, flying on a steady course at 10,000 feet, there dropped a 'stick' of bombs, each wobbling slightly before being stabilised by the fins, and then falling in rapidly accelerating and slowly expanding formation towards a line of private houses well south and east of King's Cross and St Pancras stations. As each bomb struck the ground and exploded, the flash and circular shock wave must have been clearly seen from the Heinkel's cockpit above

Joan and her relatives had been making the best of their circumstances, as usual, even though they were aware that this was a very bad night indeed. Still, there was always that illogically comforting thought that it would not happen to you. Suddenly, the crashes of the sequence of bombs, each one nearer, were terrifyingly loud. There was nothing distant and remote about them now. In those few seconds that night's raid had become entirely personal.

'You didn't move. You just heard them coming – literally – down the street,' recalls Joan.

Two of the bombs straddled the Clarke home, one in the back garden, the other in the street. One hit the building. The house was demolished. Masonry, timber and tons of bricks avalanched down the floors, most of it stopped by the cellar ceiling.

'I was protecting my mother's head,' remembers Joan. 'I had obviously just grabbed her as the bomb hit. There was a huge amount of plaster and a great cloud of soot from the fireplace as the chimney crumbled. But there were no bricks or masonry, thank God.' The five trembling women were covered in dust, but otherwise unharmed.

'When all the crashing had stopped,' says Joan, 'all we could hear was rushing water. We were in the

"Personally, Streicher, if things get too sticky I'm going to give myself up to the British and settle down in a nice country house."

Daily Express, Aug. 17th, 1944

This grim drawing shows Julius Streicher, one of Hitler's chief persecutors of the Jew, with Heinrich Himmler.

"I assure you, Herr Major, with these Americans all over the place our chance of getting a taxi is out of the question."

Daily Express, Aug. 22nd, 1944

The joke about Americans and taxis was a universal one.

"Trust honourable Fuehrer will excuse use of Western slang—but this time it seems like you've torn seat out of honourable Axis pants."

Daily Express, Aug. 30th, 1944

dark, and could very quickly feel the wet around our ankles. It was getting deeper very rapidly. We soon realised what had happened: the mains had burst.'

The women were to discover that they had been very lucky indeed. They saw that the blast had blown open the door of the room, thus saving their lives. Joan, still in her dressing gown and slippers, led her mother and aunts to the door, and they all scrambled up via a gap in the rubble through the smoking ruins onto what moments before had been Great Percy Street.

Joan recalls: 'There really wasn't a street there any more. The sky was lit up with all the fires and the bombs were still falling. It was just like you've seen in

"*Personally, Herr Schmidt, I don't think these Belgians here will support the British like the French have done.*"

Daily Express, Aug. 31st, 1944

"Well—how's Mr. Invincible this morning?"

Sunday Express, Sept. 10th, 1944

all those photographs. We were aware of what sounded like heavy rain, but it was the great torrent of rushing water from the mains. We didn't realise it at the time but the people opposite, whose house also had been hit, were being drowned. As were other neighbours. They were all friends of ours, of course. People didn't move much in those days, and we had known them all our lives.

'Their basement doors had remained shut, unlike ours, and had been blocked by the falling timbers and bricks.

'They had presumably survived the actual explosions, like us, but were trapped. They couldn't get out and where they were just filled up with water.'

The women were helped over a bomb crater, after some planks had been torn from a ruin to make a rickety walkway, by a warden. Joan remembers that as they stood waiting to be rescued there was no sense of panic or distress whatsoever.

'We all had to cross the bomb crater, one by one, and we stood there saying to each other: "After you ... no after you." It was just very English, I suppose.'

At *Reynolds News*, Giles realised that this was a particularly bad night, and that bombs had fallen over an area which included Great Percy Street.

'The thing was you usually got used to it,' he says. 'I mean it happened every night, and you could set your watch by them. You would say: "They're ten minutes late tonight." But that particular time it was bloody terrifying. Eventually I left the office and made my way slowly to Joan's house, ducking and diving in doorways.'

Joan, her mother and aunts were bundled away from the immediate danger by air raid wardens and found their way into a relatively undamaged area. The small group of deeply shocked women walked down Amwell Street into Lloyds Square and stopped,

with relief, outside the familiar and reassuring door of the local convent. Here, surely, was sanctuary both physical and spiritual.

They knocked. The large door was opened by the old caretaker, someone Joan knew, who invited the shivering and grateful group inside. There was a swish of robes and an imposing nun, presumably the Mother Superior, swept down the stairs.

'Who are these people?' she demanded. The caretaker muttered the beginning of an explanation.

'Well, they can't stay here,' said the woman of God. And thus the ladies were ushered back into the street. Stunned, they looked about them. Bombs were still falling, further away now, and flames lit up the sky to the east. Fire engines roared from street to street, bells clanging, and everywhere there were fire hoses. They had been thrown back into the full rage of the Blitz by a lady of Holy Orders. That single act had a more profound and traumatic effect than the destruction of Great Percy Street by several thousands of pounds of Hitler's high explosives. Joan Giles, who has long come to terms with the loss of her childhood home, still speaks about the incident with a sense of disbelief.

The ladies eventually found refuge at the house of a relative.

In the morning, with the grime washed from their faces though debris still in their hair, they returned to what remained of Great Percy Street to survey the wreckage of their home and to investigate the possibility of rescuing a few belongings. Joan was thinking of her fiancé. He, too, might have been bombed. He might have been killed. She borrowed some coins to telephone him, but the lines were down.

In the event, 'We sort of bumped into one another,' says Giles, 'almost by accident. There she was in the street looking awful. I'd seen the remains of the house and felt they must have all been killed.

"Suppose you cut out this 'They Shall Not Pass' stuff. Their advance patrols went past hours ago."

Daily Express, Sept. 12th, 1944

There was no one you could ask – they were all too busy looking after themselves.

'Joan wasn't hurt, as it turned out, but the doctor said she was suffering from nervous disability. But then that covered anything in those days. Her nails went black, I remember.'

I asked Joan: 'What did Carl say to you when he found you were alive and OK?'

'Oh, I don't remember,' says Joan. 'Something rude, I expect.'

Carl is quick to recall the comical moments of that morning, as they tried to recover some of their belongings from the rubble.

'I was looking into a hole in the pile of bricks and thinking of going in,' he says, 'and suddenly I saw this little figure coming out. It was Joan's mother, Agnes. She really was a very little woman. She was a jockey's daughter.

'They had hoarded lots of tins, and they were all down there in the water. So the labels had come off. You can imagine, all those tins and not knowing what was in them. You had tomato soup when you wanted peaches. For months.'

Still, Agnes Clarke was not going to be put off by the mischievous smirking of her future son-in-law. She emerged with armfuls of items from the ruins of her home, asking each family member to carry their own share. The strange little group then went in search of a room to let nearby.

Agnes had purchased some string, and tied half-a-dozen lengths from wall to wall like washing lines. The pathetic objects, most drenched in filth, were then hung up to dry.

'There was no point, really,' says Joan. 'But my mother wouldn't be beaten.'

CHAPTER THREE

To the *Daily Express*

On 14 March, 1942, Carl Giles and Joan Clarke were married at St John's Church, East Finchley. It was a cold though bright day, and a raggedy band of Home Guard chums, their bayonet tips touching to form an uncertain arch in the early spring sunshine, had turned up to do their bit as the guard of honour. At least one photograph survives, though most, taken by a photographer from *Reynolds News*, 'didn't come out'.

As the wedding preparations advanced in Finchley, the war continued, unmoved by the merry nuptials. In the English newspapers of that day, the progress of the Japanese, who had attacked the US Fleet in Pearl Harbor three months earlier and thus brought America into the war, made depressing reading. A headline read: 'Wave of Japanese Conquest Rolls On'. Under the dateline: 'New Delhi, 13 March', readers were told: 'Java, the greatest prize in the triumphant Japanese campaign of conquest in South-East Asia, has fallen. After bloody engagements in the jungle, the Dutch, British, Australian and US contingents have surrendered.' Other headlines declared: 'Washington considers Philippines lost. McArthur quits'; and 'Nurses shot in Japanese outrage'. A month earlier Singapore had fallen, a catastrophe which was described as Britain's 'Blackest Day'. In Russia, the

people of besieged Leningrad were continuing, despite terrible privations, to hold out against the Germans.

But none of this was given much consideration as the large wedding party made its way from St John's Church to the Finchley home of Joan's mother, Agnes.

Home Guard soldiers mixed with *Reynolds News* friends, Finchley neighbours and – curiously – with the members of the only complete family which had attended the ceremony. (After all, usually there were two.) As the new Mr and Mrs Giles were first cousins, it followed that only one family and no other should be involved in the proceedings.

After a noisy reception, the couple were driven to Liverpool Street station, where the whole party had gathered on the platform to wish them farewell, for a honeymoon train journey to Ipswich. The pair were forced to travel by rail, despite Giles's love of motor cars and his comfortable financial circumstances, because of the war-time petrol rationing. Still, a convenient taxi ride from Ipswich station, following a one-and-a-half-hour rail trip through the dusk of an early spring day, found them at the comfortable and imposing Great White Horse Hotel.

Says Joan: 'We stayed in the Dickens suite. I remember it had two four-poster beds.'

Following the bombing of the year before of the

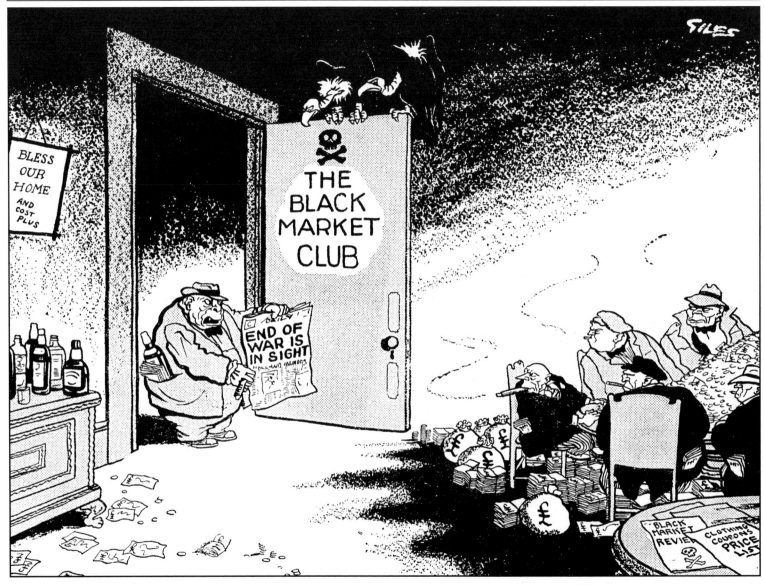

"Have you boys seen the bad news?"

Daily Express, Sept. 19th, 1944

"I know someone who'd like to be demobbed so's he could get back to his old job of house painting."

Sunday Express, Sept. 24th, 1944

Clarke home in Great Percy Street Joan and her mother had stayed with Joan's brother, Terry, in Enfield, North London. After a month they moved in to a new flat in Finchley. Giles continued to live with his mother and father in Edgware, and occasionally stayed with Joan in Finchley. Joan, in turn, often stayed with Giles in Edgware. So little had changed, really. The Giles/Clarke family continued then, as it always had done, to hold its door open to all-comers at all times. Even now, in 1994, at the Giles farm in Suffolk, the family coming and going continues, endless rounds of tea, sherry and wine adding a pleasant social flavour to the carousel.

After their marriage the couple moved to Badger's Cottage, an attractive three-bedroom house north of Ipswich which they rented from an absent naval commander. They were to move twice more, each change restricted to the same immediate area, and were to settle finally – in 1946 – in their present home, Hillbrow Farm, a few hundred yards from the village of Witnesham. So Suffolk was to be home. Suffolk, with its hardy, decent people, its estuary taverns and its chilly sailing waters, its farmers, yacht chandlers, chimney sweeps and grave-diggers, its poachers and scallywags, traffic wardens, level-crossing keepers and game-keepers, scrap-metal merchants and car-dealers – all those who were to fill Giles's bustling cartoons – was where Carl Giles and Joan would stay. For ever.

During that period of the war Giles's social and home life was dominated by his friendship with GIs. He loved Americans and, in particular, the American military. His war-time cartoons were celebrated for their depiction of cigar-chomping, grinning Yankee servicemen.

One of the most celebrated sketches, which appeared in the *Sunday Express* on 23 April, 1944 during the apprehensive months before D-Day,

concerned the Americans' infuriating talent for monopolising taxis. The old war-time cliché was that Yanks were 'over-paid, over-sexed and over here'. Nothing caused more resentment of their high-profile presence than the fact that whenever a British chap waved his brolly at a London taxi it would whiz past full of lantern-jawed, Lucky Strike-smoking American servicemen – often with pretty girls giggling on their laps and expensive perfume wafting from the windows.

Says Giles: 'The British used to think that I was being unkind. But, you know, the Americans loved my cartoons. They are cartoon people – they understood and appreciated them.'

Giles enjoyed the GIs' uncomplicated humour, their brash though engaging masculinity, their generosity of spirit, laughter, style and uniforms. East Anglia, with its numerous airfields, swarmed with them. Many drank ale in The Fountain, Giles's local pub in the village of Tuddenham. It was there that he befriended a group of black GIs who were building runways at Debach, the local USAF base. A close friendship grew, and soon the new pals were using the Giles house as a home from home, sleeping and eating there. The cosy East Anglian cottage rang nightly with a joyful blend of far-flung interests and cultures: the Deep South and Suffolk ale; Harlem and home-cooked English puddings; Dixie and – when Giles moved to that paper – the *Daily Express*; Lord Beaverbrook and Louis Armstrong.

Joan somehow managed to keep the fit frames of these splendid grandsons of sons of sons of cotton slaves well fuelled with home-concocted 'chow', despite the miseries of rationing.

'The house was full of endless laughter,' recalls Giles. 'Yes, the villagers were astonished to see these black American servicemen. They'd not seen their like before. But they took to them too. Some of the

Here is Joan with the two black GIs who became great friends of the Gileses in Suffolk. Butch is on Joan's right, Ike on her left. They were building a runway at a nearby airfield, and used to join Giles in his local pub, The Fountain, in the village of Tuddenham. There, with Giles at the piano, they formed a raggedy jazz band.

local girls even found themselves in the family way.'

The most memorable aspect of the association, one recalled with pleasure by the older taverners of those parts, was the raggle-taggle jazz band which Giles formed with his rhythmic and musical friends in the public bar of The Fountain.

Giles's friendship with the Yanks of East Anglia, black and white, became famous back home in the States. An American correspondent of the time wrote:

Giles was one of the new English humorists to seize upon the rich subject of the three million Yanks who invaded Britain during the war. A great fan of the United States, he loved American bombast and gadgetry.

He roared at the staggering variety of US army clothing but learned to draw garments down to the last seam. He loved our drooping socks, sloppy field jackets and chevrons – which seemed to the English to have as many rungs as a fireman's ladder.

When the first Americans moved into his neighbourhood near the lovely village of Tuddenham, Giles became their friend and local champion. The soldiers were members of an engineering battalion who were bulldozing, grading and levelling concrete twenty-four hours a day to get the Ninth Airforce's Marauders into the air. On Saturday evenings the negro engineers would cycle to the local pub, The Fountain, balancing bass fiddles, drums, trumpets, trom-bones and saxophones and other instruments on their handlebars.

The bass player would angle his instrument at sixty degrees in order to clear the low ceiling with its Scotch thistles, Tudor roses and *fleurs-de-lis* impressed there by Elizabethan workmen.

The Suffolk farmers would then crowd into the back room with their pints of mild and bitter as Giles struck up the opening bars on his piano and the six-piece hot band went into: 'Fat Mama With The Meat Shakin' On Her Bones'.

The joy of jazz at The Fountain was to be fairly short-lived. Giles's friends from the base were soon moved on, and contact was lost.

'They especially got on with me,' says Giles. 'They knew, you see, that their colour didn't matter a damn. They could have been black, green or blue as far as I was concerned.'

The integrated harmonies of The Fountain were in rugged contrast to the other pubs of the area.

Cockney writer Johnny Speight, creator of television's ranting working-class bigot, Alf Garnett, and one of Giles's closest friends, was himself based in the area during the war. He didn't know Giles at the time, but he tells a story which is certainly relevant to the events at Tuddenham.

'I was in a Suffolk pub one evening – I forget which it was – and there were all these Americans in there creating a bloody riot. They were objecting to the fact that one of their black soldiers had taken up with a local girl. A white girl, of course. They had

OPPOSITE: *In this photograph the characters in The Fountain include two of Giles's GI friends, Butch playing the drums and John Louis facing the camera. Standing to the right of Giles in naval uniform is local lad, Eric Ossard, known always as 'Dotsie'. These days Dotsie is Giles's chum and tireless odd-job man about the farm.*

GILES SENDS THIS FROM HOLLAND

"Unsociable lot, these Germans, sir."

Daily Express, Oct. 5th, 1944

This is Giles in his jeep with his cheery driver.

"Are you addressing ME?"

Sunday Express, Oct. 8th, 1944

Still in Holland.

"Your Missus would give you 'Vive La Belgique' if she was to come round the corner."

Daily Express, Oct. 11th, 1944

Giles spent some time recording the rejoicing in Brussels.

"Just as I expected—no hot water."

Daily Express, Oct. 17th, 1944

'im up at one end of the bar and they were going to lynch 'im. It was bloody terrifying.

'Then this village copper comes in – a real country bobby – and elbows his way through. It was almost as if he had said: "Ello, ello, ello". He hadn't even got a truncheon with him. They all fell back and it went quiet. They had been confronted by the full majesty of the law. It was amazing. He just led the bloke out. And that was before the American military police could get there with all their riot sticks and heavy gear.'

Things were to change at The Fountain, too. When the black soldiers had gone, a number of white GIs took their place. Giles had done paintings of his friends and they had been hung up in the bar. When it became clear that these pictures were going to cause offence to the white Americans, the woman who ran the establishment quickly took them down.

'It was a bloody disgrace,' says Giles.

All the while Giles had been idyllically happy working at *Reynolds News*, despite the danger and the terrifying episode in Great Percy Street. The journal was a minnow in the mighty swim of the national press, and was scarcely taken seriously by the world at large.

At the bottom of Fleet Street, only a mile away from the newspaper's modest offices near King's Cross, was the formidable *Daily Express*, a hugely successful right-wing paper at the height of its powers. It was owned by Lord Beaverbrook (1879–1964), the diminutive though dynamic Canadian, born William Maxwell Aitken, who had amassed an enormous fortune in his home country before coming to England in 1910. In 1916 he gained control of the *Daily Express* and began the *Sunday Express* in 1918, adding London's *Evening Standard* to his stable in 1923. The three journals, which successfully and eloquently trumpeted his imperialist and isolationist views to an increasingly massive audience of readers, were eventually to represent one of the greatest and most powerful newspaper publishing enterprises in history.

Beaverbrook, who was a friend of Churchill and held various cabinet posts, including that – during the war – of Minister of Aircraft Production, was a mischievous and often devilish figure. Some called him 'the little nut-brown man', and he loved to attack the establishment through cartoon and gossip column. He loved cartoons, in particular, and had a highly developed appreciation of colourful and simple visual imagery.

Meanwhile Carl Giles, a mile or so away north and west of the *Daily Express*'s ugly black glass front, continued his happy existence into the war years, drawing cartoons for the Communists' energetic and doughty Sunday voice, *Reynolds News*.

It is not difficult to imagine what Lord Beaverbrook thought of *Reynolds News* any more than it is difficult to imagine what those at *Reynolds News*, downing their pints with the dungareed printers in the Pindar of Wakefield, thought of the *Daily Express*.

Nevertheless, although Giles didn't know it at the time, the eyes of powerful men from that corner of the Fleet Street parish had been squinting with increasing interest at the particular page of that organ which

OPPOSITE: (*This is an old page from the* Daily Express *with four linked cartoons showing. The text beneath is* *included in the book. But the headline makes it self-explanatory.*)

A PAGE FROM GILES AT THE FRONT

carried his drawings. After all, his cartoons – only seen by those who read *Reynolds* or those in the newspaper trade – projected that unique sense of jokey British stoicism in a time of crisis with more spirit, humour and skilled draughtsmanship than, in the view of many, had ever been seen in the pages of a newspaper.

At this stage Giles wasn't so much poking fun at the enemy as demonstrating the cheeky disregard for danger and authority among the ordinary soldiers whom he so loved. A typical cartoon shows a couple of Tommies at the front with shells landing all about them, Germans creeping over the brow of a hill, only interested in showing each other family snaps. 'Here's a picture of my brother Fred when he was six,' says one grinning private as a howitzer shell embeds itself into the ground ten feet away.

Giles loved to dwell on the tension between the ranks. In one cartoon he shows a pretty girl in a bar observing to a group of privates: 'What! You take orders from that funny little man in the corner with the big black whiskers?' In the corner, of course, there is an English major, his 'tash points waxed to absurdly sharp points.

By this time Giles was also already achieving a necessarily limited reputation for drawing American GIs. He loved them, of course, and was so friendly with them that they would even come to London and drink in the newspaper taverns around *Reynolds News*.

One of Giles's drawings of that time was to lead to the creation of his most famous post-war character, Grandma. The cartoon shows a funny little lady with a flower on her hat giving a hard time to a couple of sentries. When you consider his work for *Reynolds*, it is not surprising that the mighty predators of the newspaper industry would soon take notice and approach him.

The first letter that arrived offering Giles a job on the *Daily Express* sat gathering dust for some days on a mantelpiece. When Giles finally noticed he tore open the envelope, read and re-read the letter, and instantly rejected the possibility of a move as entirely out of the question. He mentioned the letter to his chums in the office, and it was discussed further in the Pindar of Wakefield.

'You don't want to go to bloody Beaverbrook,' shouted his socialist chum, Gordon Schaffer, as he reached over the throng for the pints which had been assembled by the barmaid. 'Beaverbrook. My God, man, what a terrible thought.'

Others joined in. 'The Old Buccaneer. Would you believe it? Take no notice, Carl.'

'No, no, I agree,' said Giles, contemptuously. 'Kah...imagine me going to Beaverbrook. Beaverbrook of all people.'

'Anyway,' insisted another voice, probably that of Monty Slater, 'you're happy as Larry with us. You've never been so happy in your life. Take no notice, Carl. Cheers!'

'Cheers,' said Giles.

Over at the *Sunday Express* editor John Gordon, a distinguished Scot and not a man easily to be put off, contacted his boss, Lord Beaverbrook, to tell him that Giles appeared not to be in the slightest bit interested.

'We must have Giles,' replied Beaverbrook in his slightly lilting, no-nonsense voice. 'Offer him a decent wage.'

The pressure continued, and Giles, simply for the reason that he was – as Monty Slater had pointed out – happier than he had ever been, continued to reject each approach.

What finally changed his mind? Giles claims that he cannot remember precisely why or exactly when he decided to make the move, though for what could

Night thoughts of a war correspondent sleeping in a Dutch hotel which was previously occupied by the Germans.

Sunday Express, Oct. 29th, 1944

Joy Through Strength
I sketched this superman having a doze while waiting for transport to a prisoner-of-war camp behind the lines.
This is a typical Aix street scene.

Daily Express, Nov. 3rd, 1944

"Bang! And there goes the officers' mess."

Sunday Express, Nov. 5th, 1944

"Nearly had to do without a cartoon in tomorrow's paper that time, didn't they?"

Daily Express, Oct. 10th, 1944

well be the answer to the puzzle we might turn to his *Reynolds* colleague Gordon Schaffer – the man who later edited the profession's trade paper *The Journalist*.

'I think what happened is that the news editor, Arnold Russell, whom Giles didn't get on with anyway, wanted to squeeze some more news into the page. As a result he demanded that Giles's cartoon be cut down.'

This act of savagery, evidently, did not simply mean that the cartoon was reduced in size, but an inch or so of it was actually cut out. It may have been a slice of sky, a section of pavement in the foreground or a wall at the side of the picture, but whatever it was this represented to the artist an act not just of insensitivity but of brutal barbarism.

'He was furious,' recalls Schaffer. 'I think, though I cannot be certain, that this is what triggered him off.'

John Gordon remembers the struggle to lure Giles to the *Express*, and the subsequent and mysterious change of heart.

I will tell you frankly that the transfer was not an easy matter. Geniuses, as everyone like myself who has driven a team of them knows, are 'Kittle Cattle' as they say in Scotland. Sometimes you coax them, sometimes you drive them, sometimes they cry on your knee, sometimes they drive you almost to crying on theirs.

But by and large they have one attitude in common. At the start, at least, whatever change may come over them later, they are not susceptible to money persuasion. You can't bribe them.

Giles was like that. He was making very little money indeed. I took the lid off Aladdin's cave and let him peep in. All he kept saying was: 'I am very happy where I am. I would be very unhappy if I changed.'

Well, water wears away a stone. Certainly, it took much water and other liquids to wear down this particular stone, but in the end, as I determined it should be in the beginning, I transferred it from the other brook to mine.

It would probably be true to say, and I think Giles would agree with it, that having made the change he became for a time a very unhappy man. He missed the old familiar faces and the old comfortable setting. He was uncertain, diffident and thoroughly miserable.

Then all of a sudden he changed. The old certainty of touch returned. The sad grey eyes began to twinkle again behind the heavy spectacles. One day I heard him laugh uproariously at one of his own jokes.

What caused the change? The usual thing. Readers had begun to write to him in masses telling him how much they liked him.

This is not surprising. Those superb cartoons which caught so magnificently the mood of war-time Britain and which then lifted and enhanced it had suddenly a host of new admirers. A curtain had been parted on a huge stage for the talent of Carl Giles. The artist, in time, was to refer to the *Express* as his Palladium.

Giles's first cartoon for his new employer appeared in the *Sunday Express* on 3 October, 1943. Thereafter his drawings appeared regularly, for almost fifty years, once each Sunday and twice in the *Daily Express* during the week.

That first offering showed Hitler in a huge hall sitting in an armchair with the Italian Fascist leader, Mussolini, his ally, squatting at his feet at the end of a dog leash. Hermann Goering, the Luftwaffe chief, seen playing with a toy train set, is being blamed by Hitler for letting the Russians in through the back

"Hermann— you've left that verdammt door open again."

Sunday Express, Oct. 3rd, 1943

door, the Eastern Front. Swarming into the hall, of course, are the Russian hordes.

It is a good enough cartoon, a consciously political offering for his new masters, and it features, in smaller detail, much of the hilarious incidental action for which Giles's work became so rightly famous.

At that time Giles was still observing the war from the Home Front. He was not to know it, but within the year he would be rather closer to the fighting – and, indeed, to the horror – than he had ever dreamed possible.

So what was happening in Europe as Giles took up his cartooning pencil for the great Lord Beaverbrook? The Allied tanks were rolling through Italy, and the Japanese were being dislodged from areas of the Pacific. Meanwhile, the Russians were driving the occupying Germans westwards and were preparing for the final assault on Kiev, the capital of the Ukraine.

At home a report of the day read: 'The autumn harvest looks like yielding less than last year's record-breaking crop, but in most areas production remains dramatically above pre-war levels. Farmers are "digging for victory" with great success.'

And close to home for Giles, his boss was also making the news: 'After an eighteen-month absence Lord Beaverbrook has returned to the cabinet. He was named tonight as Lord Privy Seal. Churchill wants his old friend back, after letting him go last year because his feuding with Ernest Bevin, the Minister of Labour, caused friction in the war cabinet.'

Giles, having settled into his new job, also settled into a new domestic routine. He and Joan lived at Badger's Cottage near Ipswich and Giles, eventually, took to dispatching his cartoons to London by train. The war moved through the winter with increasing Allied gains, and by the late spring the talk was of D-Day, the long-awaited Normandy landings which would herald the beginning of the end for the war in Europe. Such was the operation's size that it could hardly have been kept a secret, and the newspapers were full of speculation about exactly where and when the attack would be launched.

Giles had plenty of fun as 'Operation Overlord' approached, and one of his favourite cartoons shows happy Dutchmen leaning on a wall and looking out to sea.

D-Day came at dawn on 6 June, 1944, as the greatest sea-borne invasion in world history quickly established its beachheads down the Normandy coast. On 25 August Paris was liberated. However, there was still much to do, and the Germans clung on, particularly in the lowlands of Holland and Belgium.

In early September Giles received an unexpected call from his editor on the *Daily Express*, Arthur Christiansen.

Giles caught the train to London and turned up as required outside the frosted glass of the editor's office, an imposing, brightly lit room whose large

OPPOSITE: In September 1943, Giles was lured to the Daily Express *from his beloved* Reynolds News. *There he was to stay, through war and peace, until his retirement. This was his first cartoon for his new boss, Lord Beaverbrook. The* Red Army *is streaming Westwards, and here are Stalin, Hitler and Goebbels, Mussolini – represented as a dog on Adolf's leash – and Goering as a buffoon. It was Mussolini who was Giles's favourite. When the Italian dictator was shot, the artist wrote to his wife Joan: 'I've lost my Musso.'*

"Well—what are YOU waiting for?"

Daily Express, April 19th, 1944

windows looked west up Fleet Street towards the law courts and east towards the City and St Paul's Cathedral. Giles had been in this office quite frequently, usually to be told that he was brilliant and occasionally to be informed that this view was shared by Lord Beaverbrook himself.

'Sit down,' said 'Chris'.

Giles did so, thinking that there was a tone, a mood, about this particular meeting which was quite different from any he had known before in the eleven months that he had worked for this enormously important organisation. There are times when even a constantly praised leading player in Fleet Street suddenly becomes aware of the awesome power of his employer and of his own professional mortality. Was this the sack? Surely not.

Chris leant forward. 'How would you like to be a war correspondent?'

"Do us a favour, chums—get this . . . . war over by Christmas."

Daily Express, Nov. 23rd, 1944

"Fall out the man who said 'It's a fiddle!' when the Sergeant Major drew a leave pass."

Daily Express, Dec. 7th, 1944

Giles's specs reflected the powerful light above the editor's desk, its surface the size of an aircraft carrier's flight deck. He noted the pens in the plastic mug and the three telephones. He noticed the map of the world spread on the wall, the various crayon lines in a variety of colours outlining the ebb and flow of conflict.

'What, you mean to draw?' asked Giles.

"Work it out, Len. Six sixteens is 96—that's how many quids it's going to cost you to say 'Merry Chrstmas' to this lot."
(Allied soldiers can be fined £16 for fraternising with a German.—Official)

Sunday Express, Dec. 17th 1944

Fraternising may not be quite the right word, but Giles spoke to many Germans as the Allies advanced.
He said he liked them!

'Yes, of course,' said Chris. 'Your cartoons have done so much for morale both here and amongst the troops – just think what effect they'd have if you were actually out there.'

'Fine,' said Giles, without another word.

'Good,' said Chris. 'Good. Excellent. We'll work out the details. Go off and have a drink.'

Giles, his head ringing with the implications of this unexpected departure in his ordered life, left the room. Christiansen picked up one of his telephones. 'Hello. Could you get me Lord Beaverbrook please.'

CHAPTER FOUR

Off to War

19 September, 1944. War correspondent, Captain Carl Giles, lugging a heavy khaki kitbag, clambered up the short ladder hooked on to the aft door of the DC3 Dakota transport. The aircraft was parked beside a line of others of the same type on the grass dispersal area at Heathrow, an aerodrome yet to become a major international airport. It was one of several Dakotas which would take various personnel, correspondents, officers, doctors and even entertainers to the recently relieved Belgian city of Brussels.

To the north of Brussels a day earlier, either side of the border with the still-occupied Netherlands, a massive air-borne force of Allied paratroopers, under the codename Market Garden, had been dropped or flown in by glider in order to capture bridges over the Dutch rivers near to the German frontier. It was Montgomery's gamble to shorten the war, and so it was his notion to enter Germany by its lightly defended back door. Monty declared: 'It could all be over by Christmas.' Thus, with a degree of optimism, non-combatants were being flown in.

Giles, prickly in his new battledress, was shown his position by a flight sergeant, and took his place on the canvas seating with his back to the struts of the fuselage. He had noticed with some amusement that almost all the RAF officer types he had seen so far sported the kind of moustache with which he dressed them in his cartoons. It always tickled him that 'types' seldom let you down.

Other passengers – some silent, some making jokes – were also clambering and stumbling up the dark interior to strap themselves in for the two-hour flight. The door slammed shut. After a considerable period of eerie silence, while the pilots completed their checks, the two 1,000 horse power Cyclone engines, first the port then the starboard, hissed, spluttered and finally roared with a deep throaty confidence into life.

Giles had never been abroad before. He had never been in an aircraft before. Come to that, he had never been to war before. He noticed the smell of the Dakota, a characteristic war–plane aroma, almost sweet, which combined the fragrances of oil, leather, dried sweat and vomit.

The engine growl suddenly grew to thunder. Giles, both startled and exhilarated by the volume, hung on to his straps as the Dakota, widely regarded as one of the toughest and most reliable flying workhorses of the period, accelerated down the runway and lifted up over what was still largely unspoilt farmland to the south of the A4. The aircraft banked steeply on to an easterly heading, a direction which would take it over north London and Edgware, and set course for the cold open sea and the Belgian coast.

"You know—there's something definitely un-American about you two guys at the end."

Sunday Express, Dec. 31st, 1944

Giles loved GIs. After the war, with his military fatigues, baseball cap and genuine American jeep, he drove around his Suffolk farm looking like one.

Giles sketches in a wrecked house in Belgium.

Giles looked about him at the dimly illuminated faces of his fellow passengers. Something had caught his eye – someone, perhaps. But he had definitely sensed a strange moment of familiarity as the others had settled themselves in for the flight. Then he saw: ah, so that was it.

Down at the end, his face lit by a sign near the cockpit, sat one of the most celebrated comedians of the time, Bud Flanagan, of Flanagan and Allen. The pair, with long coats and Homburg hats, who shimmied and strolled, and regularly brought down the timbers of music halls throughout the country. Flanagan was clearly off to entertain the troops.

Giles, like most of the others on the flight, fell into his own thoughts. All this was a long way down the road from Barnsbury Park School in Islington, and the class of 1927 that was terrorised by Chalkie, the schoolmaster whom Giles was eventually to revive in cartoon form and upon whom he was to wreak his revenge for the following half century.

Giles wondered what role his schoolmates, all of whom he had lost touch with, might now be taking in the war. He wondered, indeed, whether they were still alive. Where now were Mott, Gomm, Fletcher and Georgie Smith? 'My God,' he thought. 'We were frightened of Georgie Smith. He lived in a rougher road than I did. They styled you from the road you came from. You would certainly not want to face Georgie Smith if he were running at you with a bayonet.'

Giles thought of Joan, too. He was missing her already. It hadn't been an emotional parting, but then their relationship wasn't like that. They'd known each other all their lives and they had never, even when meeting amongst the rubble after the bombing of Great Percy Street, expressed any great outward demonstration of affection. It was there, but it was unspoken for much of the time.

'Take care,' Joan had said, as her husband went off to war. But she didn't shed a tear – not in public, at any rate.

The aircraft touched down lightly and taxied to a stop before the battered buildings at Brussels airport. The military were everywhere.

'All those of us in uniform marched,' recalls Giles. 'I also remember thinking: "Why are we marching?

This is bloody daft." We were fed and put up for the night. The following morning we were taken either by car or truck towards the front.'

This was the report sent back to the *Daily Express* on 18 September by Giles's travelling companion and fellow *Express* correspondent, Alan Moorehead.

FANTASTIC

We go in – swimming, bombing, parachuting, tank, jumping
Alan Moorehead: Near Eindhoven. Monday.

This is turning out to be the most fantastic battle of all. On the ground the British tanks have smashed straight into Holland, and in strength. From the air all the land ahead of us has been scattered for many miles with paratroops and with troop gliders.

On the canals the infantry is plunging ahead by swimming and by boat and pontoon bridge.

All Holland is being flung into chaos by this strange futuristic assault, in which there is no front line and in which the war is carried into three dimensions.

Giles very soon found himself in the thick of it.

He recalls: 'The noise was unbelievable. Shattering. At first all you wanted to do was dodge in and out of doorways – like in the Blitz but a bloody sight worse – and make your way to where you knew there was an HQ. Bullets seemed to be coming from every direction, which I suppose they were. The last thing that came naturally to mind was to set up an easel, get out the pencils and start drawing amusin' cartoons.'

He did draw, of course. And with one of his large

"Am I mistaken, or did I hear one of you give a long, low whistle?"

Daily Express, Sept. 21st, 1944

Arnhem – a sadly optimistic drawing. The Allies dropped into Holland in order to drive on to and through the German border. Of the bridges they had to cross, Arnhem was the bridge too far. They failed, and the whole enterprise was a catastrophe. Giles was sent out to cover the event as a war cartoonist. He then stayed on in Europe, following the Allies, until victory. He returned home in personal triumph.

envelopes of cartoons from the front he included a
brief piece of text, a letter to his readers.

This Holland...

There are many things to be said about this Holland and Nijmegen, Eindhoven, and the rest of the front-line towns and villages.

I doubt whether the average front-line soldier's comments would get past even the most broad-minded censor, but one and all agree that:

(a) It is cold.
(b) It is wet.
(c) There may be worse places.
(d) But not many.

In fact, what beats most of us around these parts is why the Germans, having been pushed nearer home, are trying so hard to come back again. I have heard certain mud-caked warriors (and Dutchmen) mutter that the Germans ought to be grateful that the Allies insisted that they — the Germans — remove their headquarters to somewhere else.

But Holland is still a good place to be. For it is a fact that whenever things are going hard, or the weather is at its worst, and conditions almost beyond enduring, you will find more genuine comradeship and spontaneous humour than at normal times.

There is always someone who says the right remark at the right time and turns the most hopeless and terrifying position into the highspot of the day.

If a shell falls rather too close and lets off a bang loud enough to shift the Houses of Parliament as far as Brighton, you will be sure to hear someone sing out: 'Stretchers!' or 'Quiet, please'.

Here are a few rough illustrations of a few actual remarks I have heard around the Nijmegen front today.

GILES

Footnote: It is even colder than I thought. Holland also has windmills.

"Advice party from the Home Front reporting, Sir."

Sunday Express, Jan. 14th, 1945

The politicians assemble before Monty and Ike.

The *Express* covered its leader page with cartoons that hilariously illustrated exactly why Giles was such a grand factor in the war effort, and in particular, how he remained such a champion of what we like to think of as the ever-cheerful, ever-resilient Tommy.

Giles never drew death, although, always to his distress, he was frequently to encounter it. He recalls the first occasion.

'There were one or two of us trying to find a quiet place for lunch – it must have been in Eindhoven or nearby – and we sat in a doorway of a collapsed building. I looked to my right and just a few feet away, half hidden behind a pile of rubble, there were four bodies.

'I went over and looked at them and immediately thought of my father. I was by his bed when he went, and had always remembered that expression left behind when life has gone. An awful emptiness.

'Some of those dead British soldiers still had their eyes half open. I covered them with their overcoats.'

As Giles and Moorehead followed the advance, it quickly became clear that the operation was turning into a catastrophe for the British up ahead. While the Americans and the Guards managed eventually to secure the bridges to the south up from Eindhoven to Nijmegen, they met heavy resistance driving north to the final bridge at Arnhem, the town where 10,000 British and Polish troops had been dropped. It was their job to take the bridge and open the way to the German border. They were surrounded and at a hopeless disadvantage.

Moorehead's euphoric report was sent without knowledge of the developing disaster some miles on.

A grim account on 20 September came from a correspondent at Arnhem itself:

After four days and three sleepless nights, Allied paratroops are holding in spite of heavy shelling

Here is Giles with two companions shortly after they landed for what was to become known as the tragic débâcle of Arnhem. What is unusual about this picture is that Giles, a war correspondent, is wearing a sidearm. He only used it, as it transpired, to disable German cars which he in later months purloined, and which he was helpfully determined to make useless to the enemy.

and repeated attacks by infantry and panzers ... in an operation dogged by misfortune, the British battle plan has fallen into German hands; it was found in a crashed glider. So when Brigadier John Hackett's 4th Parachute Brigade arrived, the enemy was waiting and picked off the men as they hung helplessly beneath their parachutes.

"I'd sooner they sent us a few pullovers instead of cartoonists."

Sunday Express, Nov. 22nd, 1944

Giles was very conscious that his cartooning pencil, however sharp, was not the most useful piece of equipment when fighting a war. However, his work was already doing a great deal for morale, both at home and at the front.

On 26 September the last British and Polish troops surrendered.

The order to abandon the operation was given by Montgomery on Monday, and the withdrawal across the Rhine took place during the night of 25–26. Only 2,400 men out of more than 10,000 who took part in the operation got away in boats or by swimming across; 1,200 were killed and 6,642 have been taken prisoner.

The ever-present Players package is tucked under his easel.

Giles and a fellow correspondent. There seems to be hardly a photograph in existence in which Giles has not got a fag in his mouth. Mind you, everyone smoked – so it seems – in the war.

Still, an advance of sorts had been made, and Giles, armed only with his cartooning equipment, had been a part of it. But already he was beginning to feel, having observed men fighting for the freedom of mankind with rifle, bayonet and grenade, that a pencil – however sharp – was not regarded by the average Tommy as of much use.

He was to be proved wrong. For his cartoons, first dispatched to London and then printed in the *Daily* and *Sunday Express*, turned up at the fighting fronts again days later as pages ripped from the journals, newspaper cuttings stuffed into letters from home, or simply by the delivery of the newspaper itself.

Study the cartoons today and they may not immediately seem to be enormously funny. But that is not the point. They caught the mood of the time, they rode the surge of that day's emotion, expressing exactly what the fighting man – infantryman, general or bomber pilot – wanted to see and hear.

Giles did a huge amount for morale. Not only did he ridicule the enemy, but he made the dangers, when faced with British spirit, appear to be inconsequential

Giles was asked to paint the colour cartoons for the front of the series of war-time 'laughs' books. There were Laughs with the Forces, Laughs with the Nurses *and laughs with just about everyone else.* The books were filled with jokes and cartoons.

Colour front and back pages for the Giles annual 1943–45.

Colour front and back pages for the Giles annual 1952–53.

Colour front and back pages for the Giles annual 1953–54.

More laughs!

"Taxi!"

Daily Express, April 23rd, 1944

This is probably one of Giles's most famous war-time cartoons. The Americans simply loved it. Giles used to explain: 'People thought I was upsetting the GIs by poking fun. But they liked it. They are a cartoon people.'

and – more importantly – extremely comical. The strange thing, as will be discovered later in this volume, is that even the enemy laughed at Giles.

Meanwhile, Giles returned to Belgium and for a while enjoyed the celebrations which by now had turned the whole of that country into a street party. Although settled into his role as a war correspondent and happily adapted to the notion of cartooning under fire, he was more than unsettled, as were his fellows, by having to wear on his helmet the white letters, WC.

'Can you imagine anythin' so daft?' he asks, his cockney always making itself apparent when indignation gets the upper hand. 'There was a lot of complainin' about it, and eventually the order came back from London that we could move the "W".

'After that we were required to go round just wearing the letter "C".

'Daft buggers.'

The Allies had made good progress in liberating Belgium, but there were still confrontations between the protagonists. One of the more notable incidents actually involved Giles, his *Daily Express* colleague, Alan Moorehead, and a couple of other correspondents whom they had briefly joined up with in pursuit of a story.

Alan Moorehead, a distinguished, urbane, tough and cultured war correspondent in the best traditions of the breed, had helped himself to a jeep – jeep-stealing was a talent Moorehead put to good use for the rest of the war – and had invited his fellows to take a day trip towards the sharp end of hostilities.

Also in the group was Chris Buckley of the *Daily Telegraph*. 'I saw a lot of Chris, though not so much as I did Alan,' says Giles. 'Chris was a tall, funny, fairly conventional Englishman, with a gentle, sensitive, amusing face. He was highly intelligent, and in some way looked like Christ.'

It was a bright autumn morning, and there was a great display of high spirits as the robust little vehicle moved at speed through the countryside. Giles, in particular, was in heaven. He was passing through a period, which was to last until well after the war, during which he enjoyed an intense love affair with jeeps. He loved any kind of stylish, mechanical conveyance, of course, but the jeep induced in him the kind of response which one associates with Toad in *The Wind in the Willows*. Giles would see a jeep roar by, and would, like Toad, sit down by the wayside, his eyes like saucers, muttering in wonderment – well, almost – 'poop, poop'. He was, one day, to terrorise his native Suffolk in just such a motor.

On this fine October day of which we speak, Giles and his companions were travelling down a straight piece of country road well to the east of Brussels, when Moorehead suddenly stood on the brakes with all the violence and strength he could muster. The jeep slewed slightly and then stopped at an angle across the road. Some fifty yards ahead, parked by a tree, was a German jeep containing four uniformed and helmeted figures. All were smoking.

As the British jeep had drawn close, one of the soldiers picked up his rifle and took aim, resting the weapon on his gloved hand which was, in turn, on the top of the windscreen. Moorehead and the others expected a bullet to zip through them. They all froze. No one moved for a full minute.

The German, who had evidently observed that Moorehead's lot were unarmed and wore the silly 'C' for 'Correspondent' on their helmets, finally lowered his rifle. Moorehead, slowly and with arms held out from his sides, climbed out of the jeep and walked at a dignified though cautious pace towards them.

Giles watched spellbound. He, too, had believed for a moment that they were all going to be shot. Moorehead arrived at the enemy's vehicle and could

"I'm n-not nervous . . . I'm n-n-not nervous . . . I'm n-n-n-not ner . . . . ."

Daily Express, Feb. 1st, 1945

Dr Robert Ley was the German Labour Front leader, and had attempted to reassure the German population as the Allies closed on Berlin.

"I don't care if the war is nearly over—I'm not selling my cab for a fiver for a souvenir."

Sunday Express, Mar. 25th, 1945

Briefly back home in London.

"And if there's any more of this hole-digging we'll take your spades away."

Sunday Express, Mar. 18th, 1945

Prisoner-of-war camps in Britain were becoming a little too jolly for the inmates and so a tightening of discipline was ordered.

"You know—there's something funny about me being here like this, and you being here like that——"

Daily Express, April 12th, 1945

be seen in earnest conversation. Hands were thrown out in positive gestures and the Germans appeared to be fascinated by whatever it was that Moorehead had to say. Suddenly, heads were thrown back and the sound of laughter reached Giles. Cigarettes were passed round. Moorehead turned and waved to Giles and the others to join him.

As Giles approached it became clear that the Germans were also newspaper correspondents. Unlike the British, they armed themselves to the eyebrows,

126

Giles sketches a cartoon, using a tank as his easel,
somewhere in Germany.

carrying rifles, sidearms and grenades. Some had been
known to use them without any provocation. Not this
lot, however. They had been so charmed by the
elegance of Moorehead's fluent German, and by the
sanguine and good-natured manner of his approach,
that they appeared to have become instant friends.

Soon Giles, who spoke not a word of German, was
joining in. Although he had a cigarette dangling from
his mouth, as he always did, he put it out in order to
accept the friendly offer of another one from the
German group's driver.

'This is Giles,' said Moorehead, in German,
'famous English cartoonist.'

'Ah, ah so – yah – so,' chorused the Germans, all

"Here come's your Easter egg.

Sunday Express, April 1st, 1945

"Sh!—We're listening to Churchill."

Sunday Express, June 5th, 1945

This kind of picture would be considered racist in these different times. Here these identical–looking Japanese soldiers, with teeth like motor-car grilles, have interrupted the broadcast of increasingly good news from home.

"Come on, Florrie, we can't wait until you see your first Red Army man—the Russians may be another week before they get to this side of Germany."

Daily Express, Jan. 25th, 1945

laughing with a combination of merry friendship and relief, as if to say that if it was left to men of humour, the world would have no need of wars.

There was something, recalls Giles, deeply touching about the encounter.

'We really thought they were going to shoot us,' he remembers. 'It was undoubtedly the cool behaviour of Alan which saved the situation. He was marvellous.

'But in a way it reminded me of that story of the First World War when, on Christmas Day, the two

"Hey you—how far is this Berchtesgaden?"

Daily Express, Feb. 6th, 1945

Stalin, Roosevelt and Churchill look for Hitler's head-quarters. On 11 February, at the famous Yalta Conference, the three were to agree to divide Germany into four zones of occupation, one each for the big three powers and a fourth for France. Berlin has now, in 1945, returned to pre-war tranquillity.

sides – only a hundred yards apart – slowly climbed out of their trenches and moved across no man's land to shake hands, then to embrace. They eventually sang "Oh Come All Ye Faithful".

'Our meeting wasn't quite like that, but there was something of the same feeling. We were enemies who

"Don't give you much time to commit suicide these days, do they?"

Sunday Express, May 31st, 1945

The American were pounding Japan. This cartoon is in appallingly bad taste, but ...

"I bet you think it funny that a bloke like me can choose wot Government I like."

Daily Express, May 23rd 1945

An embryo Giles family. The real one had yet to be created.

"Be funny if the siren went now, wouldn't it?"

Sunday Express, Aug. 19th, 1945

VE Day.

"Good-bye, sergeant, I must leave you,
though it breaks my heart to go."

Sunday Express, June 24th, 1945

"I suppose there'll soon be a lot of fuss about whether we're to fraternise with the Japs or not."

Daily Express, July 31st, 1945

Two weeks later, on 14 August, Japan unconditionally surrendered. A week earlier atom bombs dropped from American aircraft had destroyed the cities of Hiroshima and Nagasaki.

discovered in an instant that we were actually capable of being friends. It was a brief friendship of great intensity. It was strange.

'Eventually the two jeeps went their separate ways – we were at war, after all – and we waved, I remember, until we were out of sight.'

Giles remained in Belgium for some weeks, crossing the border from time to time into Holland, a country which would itself have been entirely liberated were it not for the disaster at Arnhem bridge. He was soon to experience the horror of entering Belsen with the Coldstream Guards, but knew little of the more

136

"RIGHT! FALL IN you horrible victorious soldiers before I skin the hides off you."

Daily Express, Aug. 17th, 1945

detailed, personalised and explicit cruelties of the war. However, shortly before he left Holland and moved with the advancing troops into Germany Giles was invited by his Dutch hosts to visit one of their own camps.

It was, says Giles, much like any other such camp, surrounded by barbed wire and overseen by high watchtowers. The difference was that although it had been German, it had now been taken over by the Dutch: the Dutch were the gaolers, the Germans the gaoled.

Giles was escorted around the place by a young Dutchman in a suit, and wearing rimless glasses. He looked as if he could have been a student. At each cell he would stop and invite Giles to look upon the wretched figure within. There, sitting on a board

Captain Giles and his driver, Reg Bishop, leaning against Giles's beloved jeep in a shattered corner of Brussels.

suspended from the wall by two chains, would be a German soldier – officer or otherwise – in shirtsleeves and uniform trousers, though without boots. Each unshaven prisoner had that hollow–eyed, expressionless, despairing look of the condemned man.

'In the morning,' the young Dutchman would say, pointing a skinny finger through the bars, 'he will be taken out and shot.' Giles recalls meeting the eyes of one or two of the prisoners and holding the gaze. He remembers feeling compassion. And he remembers, also, feeling a great depth of revulsion at the pleasure with which the pale–faced custodian did his rounds.

'Whenever I met people in the war I learned how all are really the same,' he says. 'They all seemed equally capable of terrible acts of cruelty, and also of being wonderfully human. It depended on which role they were playing and in what circumstances.

'Whenever I met the so–called enemy, I found it difficult, after I had spoken for only a few minutes, not to see them as I would anyone else – on Ipswich High Street, in Islington or anywhere. Equally, I was aware that those who were supposed to be on our own side could behave barbarically.'

The war, far from won, raged on through the dark winter of 1944 and into 1945. Great victories were gained both in Europe and the Pacific. At home in Britain, London and the south were to experience, come November, the horrifying assault of the V2, a rocket fired from the Dutch coast which reached the edge of space and then dropped at supersonic speed. With its inevitably indiscriminate targeting, it usually fell into civilian residential areas. Once again Joan Giles and her fellow Londoners were under savage attack.

Explained a report on 10 November, read by Giles in a tattered newspaper he found under a mug of coffee at a British HQ:

Winston Churchill at last admitted today that Britain is under attack by the secret German long-range rocket, the V2. Nearly 100 have landed since the first hit Chiswick in West London, on 8 September, but the British authorities have suppressed the information until today. As many as eight rockets a day have been launched from sites in the Netherlands – and the impact is far deadlier than that of the earlier V1, with hundreds of Londoners already killed.

Also in Britain, Laurence Olivier produced a fiercely patriotic screen version of *Henry V*, a film which he also directed and in which he starred. Joan's paper, the *News Chronicle*, was particularly uncharitable about the endeavour. Its critic wrote: 'In overbright Technicolor and half an hour too long, at its worst it is vulgar and obscure.'

The Americans fought a massive counter–offensive tank battle in the Ardennes, which became known famously as the Battle of the Bulge. In effect, though the casualties and loss of equipment were enormous on both sides, the engagement only slowed up the advance of the US forces into Germany by a few weeks.

Giles was shortly to acquire a personal jeep, thanks to the expertise of his friend Alan Moorehead, and a driver to go with it. The latter was a laconic and rather cautious Londoner called Bishop, Private Bishop, indeed. So Captain Giles, with his kitbag and drawing equipment tossed into the back, nipped about the heels of battle with a glorious sense of freedom. He had now adopted a safe routine for his drawing, and was able to judge where he might set up his temporary 'studio' and be fairly sure that he was not – as he had done so many times in earlier weeks – going to have to scarper to the safety of a hole in the ground or the protective area beneath an armoured vehicle or stationary tank.

Giles had also grown somewhat bold. And there were certain excursions into just-conquered areas of the Fatherland which Private Bishop regarded as less than agreeable.

'C'mon, mate,' Giles would say, in a manner not usually associated with that which marks the relationship of officer and foot-soldier, 'let's go down there. It looks quiet enough.'

Bishop would look ruefully down the street, where half the buildings had tumbled and slithered into rubble, and where dark and acrid smoke would often

"I'm afraid you'll find Sir Edward a little touchy—our young visitors dressed him up for
VJ day and we can't get it off."

Sunday Express, Aug. 26th, 1945

"Sh! Listen! I've got Tommy Handley!"

Sunday Express, Nov. 25th, 1945

Youngsters will have no idea who Tommy Handley was. Starring in a radio show called ITMA – abbreviation for 'It's That Man Again' – he was a much-loved wireless comedian back home in Britain. The notion that he may have been picked up at the Nuremberg Trials, those proceedings which brought justice to the surviving monsters of the Third Reich by the headset-wearing Rudolf Hess, must have been regarded as hilarious by Handley fans.

still be drifting slowly across the silent ruins, and say: 'You must be jokin', sir.'

'C'mon, mate, let's give it a go,' Giles would urge.

'Don't say I didn't warn you, sir,' Bishop would say, engaging first gear. And off they would go, flying like the devil. If their jeep was going to be a target, then it was going to be one that dodged and darted and moved like the ruddy wind. In fact, the pair often came across rather disconsolate-looking Germans, some walking, some sitting in doorways.

'Actually, they usually saluted,' recalls Giles.

At one small town, the name of which Giles cannot recall, he told Bishop to pull up at a reasonably prosperous-looking house on the main street. A middle-aged woman stood in the doorway, and Giles was keen to speak to anyone for whom the war was so recently over.

The woman spoke English, and invited both Giles and Bishop into the house. There they discovered a large family of women assembled in the main room.

'Please,' said the older woman, motioning them both to seats.

What followed was yet another experience of the war which Giles found at once confusing and encouraging. Both generations of the family – educated, cultured middle class and gently hospitable – spoke reasonable English. They soon engaged Giles in earnest discussion about the war and about the British, about Churchill and about Hitler, about death and triumph and defeat. There was no bitterness, only a kind of dignified sorrow and profound weariness. And now, perhaps, relief.

The father of the house, it transpired, was away fighting in the navy. They had little money and few provisions, but Giles and his driver were most welcome to stay for dinner, and indeed for the night. There were spare rooms and fresh linen.

'It was very strange,' remembers the artist. 'We were a conquering army racin' through their country. There was destruction everywhere. Yet they made us as welcome as if we had been long-lost relatives. These people weren't the enemy, they were just people.'

It is doubtful, it should be said, whether bespectacled, unarmed Giles with the strange letter 'C' on his helmet, and his friendly driver, Bishop, ever looked very threatening to anyone. But they nevertheless wore the uniform of the conquering army.

Whatever the reason, as winter darkness closed over the German town that evening, the squeak and clatter of tanks now gone and the rumble of the guns growing distant like a storm which has passed on towards the mountains, the lamps burned long and bright around the large front parlour of the German home in that crumpled street. The hostess and her family talked of war and of the husband away at sea, and of those who had died and of those who might come home; Giles talked of Ipswich and the estuary and the taverns, and of going back. And of peace. And he dipped into his kitbag and showed them his drawings. He showed them his cocky Tommies with their cheeky faces and his square-jawed Germans with their square-built helmets. And he showed them a sketch of his preposterous Hitler, scampering for shelter, bullets whizzing round his ears.

The family smiled. For now they dared.

OPPOSITE: Giles and Bishop on the wreck of a German anti-aircraft gun outside Brussels.

An unnamed German family befriended by Giles somewhere near Hamburg. They took him in, fed him and gave him a bed.

As the Allies fought their way into the German heartland they were to discover the truly evil nature of the Third Reich. Soldier fought soldier with all the savagery of war. There were few rules in the blaze of battle. On the field of conflict, ruthlessness, cruelty and appalling brutality were part of the contract. But few warriors, however hardened, were prepared for the ghastly horrors of the concentration camps.

It was the Russians, advancing from the east, who were the first to come face-to-face with what later was to be termed the Holocaust.

The following is a newspaper report, read some days later by Giles and his comrades-in-uniform on the Western Front, filed from Auschwitz-Birkenau on 27 January, 1945.

At midday, the four young Soviet cavalrymen, guns at the ready, came cautiously down the road that

"HE WAS ALWAYS SO KIND TO ME AND THE THREE CHILDREN." (Kramer's wife)
"Now, if you're all very good Daddy will tell you a story about the good fairy who put ten thouand people in the gas chamber."

Sunday Express, Sept. 30th, 1945

When Giles entered Belsen concentration camp with the liberating soldiers of the Coldstream Guards, he spent some time, he recalls, interviewing the commandant, Josef Kramer. A ceremonial dagger and swastika armband which he keeps in a box in his Suffolk farmhouse were given to him by Kramer before the Nazi was marched away under arrest. Kramer, says Giles, knew and admired his cartoons.

surrounded the camp. Looking through the barbed wire, they saw living skeletons moving slowly in a landscape of corpses sprawled in the snow, punctuated by broken-down and burnt huts. The Red Army had stumbled on the Nazis' biggest extermination camp.

As the booming of the Russian artillery came nearer, the Nazis attempted to conceal the traces of their hideous mass murder. They have burnt most of the camp's carefully maintained records. Nine days ago they evacuated the twenty thousand prisoners with the most chance of survival. Those who were too weak to walk from the camp were shot dead. The rest have been dispersed to other camps further West. Anyone falling behind on the long march to their new destination was shot and thrown into a ditch.

Giles was not to know it as he shared his revulsion and incredulity with his fellow correspondents, but he – and they – would themselves shortly be looking through the barbed-wire gates of another demonic outpost of that hell. And they were to witness far worse than the Russians.

Their erratic route through Germany was to take them to Belsen, a camp from which the evil custodians had not fled, a death factory which appeared still to be in full production. The unbelieving troops lined up along the perimeter fencing, and their officers focused their binoculars on the trains, their locomotives half hidden in steam, which had just brought the latest cattle-wagon consignment of Jews, gypsies and the insane for gassing and incineration. It was as if the diabolical dedication of the work, and the sheer volume of the task which confronted them, was such that the participants were incapable of understanding the nature of what they did.

Although Giles now preferred to move about independently whenever possible, he spent much of his time in the company of the *Daily Express*'s Paul Holt, the newspaper's former film critic. It was the celebrated editorial policy of Lord Beaverbrook – and thus of his editors – to give what appeared to be entirely inappropriate jobs to the most unlikely of reporters. It had the effect of producing a startlingly fresh view of things, and sometimes led, as it did with Holt, to inspired and memorable war reporting.

Recalls Giles: 'I liked him. He was a funny man. Unusual. He was of average height, though there was not one ounce of him that you would describe as being like a soldier. He could observe aggression with satisfaction, but would never indulge in it. Paul had a soft manner of speaking, but was what you might call quietly supercilious – he couldn't help, when he addressed you, but talk down his nose. He spoke posh, but he was a knowledgeable, even learned man. Sometimes when you saw him watching something unpleasant, you had the impression that he was enjoying it. He could be rather sinister. In a curious way we got on rather well.'

Thus it was that this unlikely pair – film critic and cartoonist, both faintly awkward and uncomfortable in their military uniforms, both newspapermen whose role had always been to communicate with their readers on the lighter aspects of life, enthralling them with the gloss and glamour of the glittery screen or lightening their spirits with the magic of the artist's cartooning pencil – found themselves in mid-April, 1945 gazing through the wire of Belsen extermination camp.

'The Coldstream Guards had gone in and we remained on the outside,' remembers Giles. 'Life inside seemed to be going on as normal. You could actually hear the screams and the shouting, from what I suppose you would call the depot, where a train full of prisoners had just drawn in.

'All you could do was look and just try to absorb what you were seeing.'

From left to right: unknown newspaper man, Reuters correspondent, Des Tighe, Aussie correspondent, Ronnie Monson, Giles and fellow Express*man, Paul Holt, film critic turned war reporter. Tighe, says Giles disapprovingly, used to be a boyfriend of Joan. Monson was a fierce Australian with a quick temper. When he saw a gross German laughing in a hunting lodge near Belsen he beat him up in the bar before a startled crowd of locals. The equine cartoon on the wall behind Giles features a celebrated hero of those times, Tishy, the creation of artist Tom Webster, also a correspondent from London and chum of Giles.*

Giles remembers that the day was very hot. It was a spring heatwave. There was stillness, and you could hear the flies and the distant bark of dogs. You could hear an occasional clatter from the distance as if someone had dropped a large plank of wood off a roof, and the occasional short toot of a locomotive's

"Catch, Eddie!"

Daily Express, Aug 8th, 1945

The 'bomb' was now to feature terrifyingly in the Cold War, of course. It was, for a long time, treated as a joke. Neither Giles nor anyone else realised just how close the world was to come to destruction as the Soviet Union and the West stood in tense confrontation for much of the remainder of the century.

whistle. You might, recalls Giles, have been on the outskirts of a town, witnessing the innocent bustle of everyday life.

'I'm not goin' in there,' said Giles quietly.

Paul Holt looked at him and back across the endless lines of huts where figures shuffled and jerked from the doors to observe, to take in what they most probably didn't believe – that the outside world had come to rescue them.

After a while he said: 'You have to go in, Carl. We both have to. It is important that we see it so that we can pass it on. Tell the world. We have a duty. We have to go in. We really do.'

Giles looked about him. He felt the heat of the sun on his back. This was the weather of his Suffolk childhood, the sort of day when, visiting his parents' farming family as he often did as a boy, he had seen the corn stand still and blaze with gold. This was the heat, too, of Chalkie's classroom. Windows open, equations squeaked onto the blackboard, thoughts far away.

Nothing moved, not a bird in the hedgerows. This was the glorious weather of the summer harbour, yachts' sails listlessly searching for the lazy wind, girls on decks, shirtless men perspiring as they paddled their dinghies here and there. Dogs yapping at the water's edge.

Halcyon days they were called. Until now.

"Get that nasty thought out of your mind, Wilson."

Daily Express, Aug. 30th, 1945

In Rangoon, Burma, the Japanese forces, still with their teeth to the front, march to sign a formal surrender under the eye of Australian troops. This cartoon is the favourite of Giles's friend, comedian Michael Bentine. Having not seen it for years he was not only able to describe it exactly but remembered the caption, word for word. And he rendered it in a wonderfully slow and lazy Aussie accent.

There was almost nothing that Giles had seen in the whole of his life which could not be cheered up with a stroke of the pen. Until now.

Said Holt: 'When you see this in the papers back home you won't want to believe it, any more than will the readers. We have to confirm to them that this place existed. We must go in.'

Giles nodded and the two correspondents walked with dread towards the entrance, a huge barbed-wire gate framed in a red-brick arch where men of Her Majesty's Coldstream Guards had taken up sentry duty.

Giles, who says that not a day goes by when he does not think of Belsen, admits that the horrors he looked upon in that place were both beyond his own words and beyond the will of his cartooning pencil.

'What could I have drawn,' he asks, 'that would have told anything more vivid than the dreadful photographs which continue to haunt us? If you want to know, look at those. Read the newspaper reports of the time. The impressions are fresh.'

In the days that followed, the people of Britain were to read the following:

There is a pile of naked female corpses here, 80 yards long by 30 yards wide and four feet high. You can't see any faces; just bony elbows, knees and buttocks or twisted hands and feet. It looks like the overladen counter of an insane butcher's shop where flies dance on the mound of greying flesh.

It is two days since the British army agreed a truce with the local German commander which enabled them to enter the camp peacefully. The Hungarian armed guards who stayed on duty 'to prevent a mass break-out', have shot dead 83 prisoners for minor offences. Now the British are in full control, and a Jewish sergeant, Norman Turgel, has arrested Josef Kramer, the camp's commandant.

During the uneasy period between the British army's arrival at the vast camp and the point at which they had taken control, Giles and other correspondents had sought out Kramer and had attempted to interview him. He had been attacked by a number of Guardsmen, and though he was still partially in charge he made no attempt to defend or even to excuse himself. The impression gained by many of those observers who had entered the camp was that the custodians had become unaware – or perhaps had always been unaware – that they might be engaged in terrible evil. The women guards, recalls Giles, were still walking around with whips hanging by straps from their wrists.

Kramer, too, was still in possession of his sidearm when Giles was shown into the room where he had been asked to stay put by the still bewildered Guards officers. He was to have a surprise for the bespectacled cartoonist who stood both fascinated and horrified before him.

'He was a handsome, swarthy man with a slight smile,' remembers Giles. 'I remember thinking after I had spoken to him for a while that if you didn't know what he had been responsible for you would

OPPOSITE: This is Ronnie Monson, the fierce Australian Reuters correspondent, who attacked a bloated German huntsman near Belsen. Giles renamed him 'Monsoon'.

have thought that he was a rather charming and cultured man. Mind you, I had more reason than others, perhaps, to think so.'

Giles recalls his moment of introduction.

'My name is Carl Giles,' he had said. 'I am a cartoonist for the London *Daily Express*.'

Kramer had looked at him in surprise. 'I know your work,' he said in clear and fluent English. 'So, you are the great Giles. That is amazing. I have seen many of your cartoons of the war. They are excellent. Please, whatever happens, I would be very honoured if you could send me an original ...'

At this moment two tough Guardsmen, their features twisted with anger, came crashing through the door. They took up menacing positions on either side of Giles, who was certain that they were going to beat him to the floor. They looked at Giles, who stood silently, and looked back at Kramer. He remained impassive.

'Bastard,' exploded one of them. 'We'll be seein' you later.' Perhaps it was the senior rank of the German which stayed their hand. Still, Giles knew they meant it. He had already seen and heard the result of the British soldiers' fury. Some of the guards had been so badly beaten that they were unrecognisable. Some, without question, were dead. These things were accepted by all, and most of these incidents were not even reported.

Alone again with Kramer, Giles was able to consider the extraordinary fact that this terrible man – or this man who had been directly responsible for one of the most disgusting outrages in the history of mankind – was actually a fan of his work. Kramer gave a faint, apologetic smile, ludicrous – even surreal – under the circumstances.

'Of course I'll send you an original,' said Giles, aware of the almost absurd nature of the conversation.

'Perhaps I can give you a souvenir,' said Kramer.

So saying, the German commander of Belsen unstrapped his Luger pistol, slid the small ceremonial dagger off the belt at his hip, pulled the scarlet and black swastika band off his upper arm and placed them all together on the table.

'Take these,' he said. 'I shall not be needing them any more.'

Giles wrapped the pistol and holster, dagger and scabbard in the armband. 'Thank you,' he said. And thus it was that the objects of rank of Josef Kramer, once a proud officer of the *Wehrmacht*, found their way into Giles's kitbag.

'I have to say,' recalls Giles, 'that I quite liked the man. I am ashamed to say such a thing. But had I not been able to see what was happening outside the window I would have said that he was very civilised. Odd, isn't it? But maybe there was a rather dishonourable reason. I have always found it difficult to dislike someone who was an admirer of my work. And strangely, Kramer was.

'I never sent him an original. What was the point? He had been hanged.'

In the following days reports from the camp continued to horrify the world. The *Express* told its readers:

Kramer's men have been disarmed. They have been put to work burying the estimated ten thousand dead lying around the camp. They have to be locked up to prevent them from the vengeance of the prisoners. Yesterday, seven 'Kapos' (prisoner guards) were savagely beaten to death.

About 30,000 victims, mainly Jews, gypsies and political prisoners, are still alive, but raging epidemics of typhus and dysentery threaten to finish off the deadly work that the Nazis started. British medical staff are now struggling to save lives and halt the spread of the disease.

"On the fifth step in May 1536 Anne Boleyn paused on her way to the block—and on the sixth step in May 1941 me and my mates put out a couple of incendiaries." *(The Tower of London is now reopened to the public)*

Sunday Express, Jan 6th, 1946

The Tower of London, which was closed in the war, was still guarded by the quaint but ever courageous Beefeaters.

Giles and Holt, aware that they were in the centre of one of the most historic horror stories of the war, remained in the area of Belsen for some two weeks. They spent as much time away from the camp as they could, and even sought some kind of social life in and around the local town in order to take their minds off the infamy down the road.

By now Giles and Holt had befriended an Australian correspondent called Ronnie Monson. They found one or two hostelries around Belsen which served excellent beer and where their presence was treated with the sullen deference to be expected by an occupying army. One such establishment was the local hunting lodge, an impressive wooden building with huge open fires and antlered trophies and wild boar heads lining every wall. The trio had quite taken to this place, and regularly occupied one end of the long panelled bar.

Monson, more than the others, found it difficult to take his mind off the grotesque images which had confronted them at the camp, and was in an almost permanent state of deep anger. He was a small, wiry chap with incredibly fierce eyes and a savage temper, whom Giles had drawn, at some stage, as a ferocious-looking human head perched on a whirlwind. There was little doubt that in those days after Belsen Ronnie Monson was a man looking for trouble: he found it.

One evening, Giles, Holt and Monson were sitting on their usual perch when the door flew open and a stout German in plus-fours and heavy leather hunting jacket strode in followed by some cronies. He banged the bar and roared an order at the barman. Monson narrowed his eyes.

The German then sat on a stool, his friends about him, and exchanged what must have been stories of a ribald nature. Every thirty seconds he would throw his head back, roar with laughter, then raise his huge pewter beer flagon until his bulbous snout and huge red cheeks had entirely disappeared. When his features re-emerged his mouth would be rimmed with foam which he would then wipe off savagely with the sleeve of his leather jacket.

Giles and Holt were now watching Monson with fascination. He placed his beer carefully on the surface of the bar and was staring at the German with a terrifying intensity. One more brutish roar from the other end of the bar was enough. He stood up and walked slowly down the line of stools until he stood before the huntsman. Although his target was some inches above him he swung his right fist and made enormously powerful contact, smack in the middle of the German's face. The nose and lips spread horribly under the impact, and the vast man swayed backwards on his stool, his left hand grasping at the bar for support. Smack. Monson's second punch landed about three seconds after the first. The German swayed again, his purchase on the edge of the bar loosened and his fingers slid and gave way. There was a sickeningly loud thump and clatter as man and stool parted company and fell to the hunting lodge floor.

The German, blood running from his nose, half sat up. His friends had backed off and were watching in astonishment. Monson leapt astride the groaning figure and piled punches into him, left and right, until his grunts had turned to pleas for compassion. Monson delivered a final right hook to the side of the German's head and jumped back, standing legs astride, fists still clenched, about three feet from him. The German half lay, his huge hands held up before his blood-smeared face.

Recalls Giles: 'It really was the most amazing sight. Monson was only a little sod, but he was terrifying when upset. I remember, in particular, the expression on Paul Holt's face. He had obviously enjoyed every second of it. He had that half-smiling look of sadistic satisfaction.

'To tell the truth,' said Giles, 'we all felt better – especially Ronnie.

'Actually, the British and the Australians showed a great deal of restraint. We heard some days later that when the Americans had gone into Dachau they simply shot any German they saw.'

A report datelined Dachau, 29 April, read:

Enraged GIs who liberated Dachau death camp today killed any SS guards crossing their paths, including at least 122 who had surrendered. At Webling, about five miles away, 43 SS men were killed.

The GIs, men of the 157th and 222nd Infantry regiments, found mounds of bodies outside a crematorium, and lying inside and alongside rail cattle trucks. Local civilians were busy looting accompanied by their children. An arrogant commander attempted a formal military handover. The GIs screamed: 'Kill 'em,' and opened fire. Eighty died before a colonel intervened.

At Belsen, the British troops, with the help of doctors and nurses, were beginning to sort out the desperately sick from the merely skeletal. The latter, it was decided, were well enough to be given a party. Thus, on the orders of a senior officer, a dance was arranged for them in the local town hall.

Remembers Giles: 'Soldiers were told to go to all the homes around and about and get hold of smart evening suits and ballgowns. Huge hampers of garments were collected, and the former prisoners tried them all on until they found clothes which would roughly fit. Of course, everything was much too big.

'We were all asked to the dance.

'The regiment provided a small band, and we all did our best to join in. I remember dancing with one or two of the women and all I could feel were the bones in their skinny little hands and their almost bare ribs and sharp shoulder blades.

'It was, truly, a *danse macabre*. It was a terrible idea.

'But they were free. And alive.'

CHAPTER FIVE

To Victory

Before long, Giles – with more relief than he could remember – left the stench of that God-forsaken place behind. He and his driver, Reg Bishop, had parted company, and the cartoonist captain no longer had a jeep. So he simply stole any car he could lay his hands on. This sounds a little shocking, but it had quickly become custom and practice; the helping of yourself to anything you fancied was regarded as being entirely in order, and no one ever mentioned that nasty word 'looting'.

'I nicked a whole lot of cars,' admits Giles. 'I had a lovely little open sports Mercedes for a while – it was late spring and the weather was glorious – but that was nicked back by another German, the sod. So I just found another one – but it was no real replacement.'

The recollections of Giles concerning his informally acquired trophies of war produce absolutely no sign of shame whatsoever. So I pressed him further.

'Oh, I had everything,' he says. 'I had the most expensive camera you could imagine. And watches and binoculars and radios and antique objects and even a violin from a bombed-out house. In fact I had so much that when I eventually got back to the coast, they refused to take me on an aircraft and suggested that I go back by boat. Which I did.

Giles fired a few bullets into this German car. He had stolen it – as he had stolen many others – and now wished to render it useless to the enemy.

GILES GOES WITH THE BRITISH

"All right, all right—
—keep yer 'air on—I've seen yer"

Giles admits to looting, or 'helping himself', which everyone did, apparently. The cartoonist came back bent low under cameras, binoculars and all kinds of German-crafted gadgetry. He also returned with a fine pair of shoes for Joan, which he 'found' in a shop. They had actually, at one stage, been stolen from him, 'nicked' from his kitbag: he nicked them back. The activity was entirely shameless.

INTO GERMANY

"me sir? looting sir?"

'One of the most important things I got hold of were a pair of beautiful shoes which I found in a shop. I got them for Joan.

'You wouldn't believe what happened. There was this little fart from Reuters called Doon Campbell – a little sneak of a man – and he pinched the shoes when I was asleep. I knew he had done it the next morning. I could tell by the look on his face.

'I went straight to his kitbag and took the buggers out.'

As Giles drove happily through the ruins of Germany, following in the tank tracks of the advancing Allies, he continued to arrange for his endless production of cartoons to be flown back to England. They were by now almost all celebrating the victory of the Tommy over the Kraut. There were all kinds of pictures of dishevelled and depressed-looking German infantrymen, with bony faces and large chins showing gloomily under their coal-bucket helmets, as they straggled through forest and wilderness, or skulked in the doorway frames of shattered buildings. They were seen scuttling out of the way of cheery Cockneys and cheeky Northerners, and were generally given a very hard time by the enthusiastic tip of Giles's cartooning pencil.

As I have said before, many of these cartoons are not particularly funny to those who study them all these years later. They certainly don't produce a howl of laughter. But it is necessary to see them, if possible, through the eyes and hearts of the British civilians and servicemen of the time. The pictures, gloriously well drawn, showed the British and their allies marching to victory, and achieving triumph in splendidly cheerful and honourable style. And they showed, at the same time, the ugly and evil Kraut, either cowering or on the run, as a preposterous and laughable enemy in defeat. That's what the *Daily Express* readership wanted. And that's what they got.

159

Giles receives direction. Hamburg, says the sign, is 18 kilometres.

What is interesting about Giles's war work is that it allows us, after a period of studying it, to share almost exactly the emotions of fifty years ago. These cartoons were universally acclaimed, bringing a tremendous sense of joy and relief after four-and-a-half years of fear. The headlines still spoke of death and of a continuing battle, but Giles's cartoons showed it in simple terms. We had won, and the Hun was on the run.

Giles had also had a tremendous amount of

GILES DREW THESE IN THE DRIVE ON BREMEN

"I warn you – I'm terrible when I'm roused – so no tricks."

"Well – how do you like your life under the British?"

enjoyment creating caricatures of the main protagonists. He occasionally drew Montgomery, Churchill or Eisenhower, but he created his most successful mischief with comical likenesses of Hitler and his henchmen, Goering, Goebbels and others, and with Mussolini.

'I called him Musso, and really got to like him. If you draw funny versions of bad people – if you remove the evil – then you can develop a great affection for them. I even liked Hitler, in a way, because I drew him as a funny little man who was always in disastrous circumstances, being let down by fools.

'Musso I sometimes saw as Hitler's pet dog, always on the end of a leash. I think Musso was my favourite, really.'

This cosy association was to end very suddenly. And there was nothing amusing about it when it came. The reality was not the stuff of cartoons. Hitler died on 30 April, 1945.

The newspapers of that day reported:

Hitler spent the last days in the Berlin bunker ranting about the betrayals, cowardice and lies all about him.

"Bah! The world's going soft, sir. We managed our wars without atom bombs in my young days."

Sunday Express, Feb. 24th, 1946

"That's handy—here comes the chap who shares your garage."

Daily Express, Mar. 19th, 1946

It is funny to reflect that even today eccentric collectors of World War Two vehicles still clutter their drives and infuriate their neighbours with these ugly and long-redundant contraptions.

The end came this afternoon. According to survivors, who escaped while the Russians were virtually hammering on the Chancellery doors above ground, the Führer slipped away to his room. Minutes later a shot was heard. Members of his staff found him on a sofa, dead from a gunshot wound to his mouth, a revolver on the floor.

These were liberated Russian prisoners at a Red Cross hospital near Osnabruck in Germany. Each of the men is a victim of German brutality. Giles is talking to the man *on crutches who had his leg forced between the bars of a gate and who was then bent backwards until the bone broke.*

Eight days later, Joan Giles, back in England, was to read in her paper: 'Mussolini and his mistress, Clara Petacci, were shot by Italian partisans today, and strung up by their heels from the façade of a petrol station in Milan's Piazza Loretto.'

Giles wrote the same day to his wife: 'I have lost Musso.'

So, one by one, Giles was indeed to lose the characters which had bustled about in his own creation, his own variation, of a world at war. It was a personal loss, the significance of which only a cartoonist, an artist who has the licence to imbue monsters with innocence and magic, could properly appreciate.

There was an exception. Just one of the grim set of characters who had served Hitler so well could not, in Giles's view, be transformed or adapted happily to his merry landscape: Heinrich Himmler. It was Himmler who was the chief architect of the Nazi terror, and dedicated exterminator of the Jewish people.

'He wore half-moon glasses and never removed his peaked hat. He was very self-conscious about his baldness. I hated him. He was the most chilling of the leading Nazis, and there was no way I could find a way to try to be funny about him. So I just drew him as he was.'

It is ironic that the only one of his war characters that Giles actually saw in the flesh was Himmler. It was the third week of May, and Himmler had gone on the run. He knew that if he were caught there could only be one fate. Arrested by a British patrol in Hamburg, he was taken to the Second Army HQ at Luneburg Heath. He was locked up while it was decided what to do with him.

Giles, along with other correspondents, had heard that Himmler had been captured, and was keen to have a look at him. HQ staff said that this would be possible, and suggested that he come along the following day.

That same night Himmler was examined by a doctor. He was, in fact, being searched as much as examined. For there was the fear, when any of Hitler's henchmen were captured, that they would take a cyanide pill and thus evade trial for undoubted war crimes.

The doctor stuck his index finger in Himmler's mouth, but was not quick enough. The German jerked his head back, bit on the poison phial and collapsed within seconds. Despite stomach pumps and emetics he died. He was left, where he had fallen, until he could be seen by a Red Army liaison officer.

'I was told he was dead that same evening, and went along to the HQ,' recalls Giles. 'There were people around and much excitement. Everyone was havin' a look.

'I pushed past a group of British officers and stood in the door. It was difficult not to be fascinated. I had drawn this man and there he was – dead, but looking exactly as I had always imagined him. He still had his hat on, I remember, even in death.'

Viscount Montgomery had said: 'The forces surrendering will total over a million chaps ... and that, gentlemen, is a good egg ...'

Moments earlier, Monty, in a tent on desolate Luneburg Heath to the north-east of Hamburg, had played host to the surrendering German high command. It was 4 May, 1945. Giles, with sketch pad, was there.

After all the destruction, the formally polite ceremony of signing the surrender that evening in the bleak light of a single bulb looked more like an investiture at Buckingham Palace. Giles had found himself a position near the tent opening, and had heard the crunch of approaching feet. The generals,

Montgomery: ". . . The forces surrendering will total over a million chaps . . . and that, gentlemen, is a good egg . . ."

Daily Express, May 8th, 1945

Giles was witness to the surrender by German generals and admirals at Luneburg Heath, where a stern-faced Montgomery presided. Giles was amused by Monty's quote of the time.

"If they did away with wars there'd be no need for Victory Parades."

Sunday Express, June 9th, 1946

The victory parade was a magnificent affair – the nation went potty.

1940 . . . Battle of Britain Week . . . 1951

Sunday Express, Sept. 9th, 1951

who had arrived in their staff cars, were being escorted to ignominy. Monty was waiting for them, the expression on his face closer to the sternness of a headmaster rather than the arrogance of a conquering war lord. Officers and aides stood about looking frightfully serious, but feeling little but euphoria.

'It was a very English occasion,' remembers Giles. 'The Germans were suddenly face-to-face with what had defeated them: the British. But there was something entirely English about it. Many of the witnesses, with their grave officers' faces and moustaches and funny thin noses, were like characters out of a film made at

168

Ealing studios. I drew several pictures of Monty. He was very easy. He was just a long knobbly nose, a black beret and heavy sort of duffle coat. The Germans wore great coats, some those shiny leather ones.

'It was all very sombre. And you didn't really think of what a moment of history you had been some small part of until later.

'When Monty read the surrender terms to the Germans it was almost as if he were declaring a list of new school rules.'

And so Giles hung about Hamburg and enjoyed the considerable hospitality of the British forces. As soon as they knew who he was he became warmly and generously fêted.

'I say,' officers would announce, 'you see that man in the corner over there with a sketch pad? Well, that's Giles. Would you ruddy well believe it? Let's have him along to the mess this evening. Give 'im a party.'

And so it was that the last days of Giles's war in Europe were spent very much as many of the intervening days had been spent, toasting whatever there was to toast – in this case, peace – with the best alcoholic beverage available.

It was then time, finally, to head home. Now he could think, freely and without that uncertain regard for the future that all war brings to even the most adventurous and optimistic mind, of Ipswich and late summer days on the estuary, of The Fountain and The Maybush. And of Joan.

'There was an army dispatch rider called Bill Hollingsworth,' says Giles, 'a Londoner. He was a decent bloke, not loud, but he laughed a lot – laughed, that is, when he was meant to laugh, when things were genuinely funny.'

Giles has always judged men by the manner of their laughter.

'Bill rode a Harley Davidson like the devil himself,' says Giles. 'Still, I was happy with motor bikes, even

Here is Giles at Luneburg Heath just after the signing of the surrender and preparing to return to Belgium with this impressive-looking dispatch rider. His name was Bill Hollingsworth, and even though Giles was once a motorcycle fanatic himself, he was given a ride of sheer terror. 'We would go straight at a war memorial in some town and just dodge past it at the last moment,' remembers Giles.

"What's this? 'Darling Basilkins, You remember when the feelthy British here was last time well I am still live in the same little house in Cairo if you care to give me a call when you come again yes please, Your own little Cleo.'"

Daily Express, Aug. 16th, 1956

Egypt's president, Colonel Nasser, had nationalised the Anglo-French-controlled Suez Canal Company. Neither Britain nor France sought to hide their anger at the Egyptian dictator's arbitrary action in laying hands on the vital lifeline for oil supplies to Europe. Military action was threatened – and eventually taken – much to the outrage of the United States. And much to the outrage too, of Giles.

FEELTHY GILES CARTOON?
(WITH CAPTION BY NASSER)

Yesterday's news that Nasser was re-printing *Daily Express* cartoons with captions altered to the pro-Nasser line brought mixed feelings to this department.

First reaction was to rush in to the editor and demand a wage increase, but reading on and coming to the piece which went: "In some cases the Arab caption writer may have been making an honest attempt to translate an untranslatable English joke" made us pause.

Loose remarks like this are apt to make a sensitive editor start asking why he has been paying us all these years for untrans-latable jokes.

A suggestion to flout the Nasser caption writers was that all future cartoons published in the Express should be printed with 100 per cent pro-Nasser captions in the hope that in translation Nasser might find himself handing the Arabs a 100 per cent line of British propaganda.

However, until a retaliation campaign has been decided on, the examples below show what is going on. The original caption is printed in heavy type with the Nasser translation below.

"My damn feet are playing up Old Harry."
Translation
"Soon the little boots I will put on and kick the feelthy British out of Suez."

"Oh, dear, this is the 53rd cold this summer."
Translation
"Oh, dear, I hope Colonel Nasser doesn't stop smelling salts and aspirins coming through the Canal."

"I want my dinner."
Translation
"We want Nasser."

Daily Express, Aug. 28th, 1956

Giles has fun with the crisis.

"Who's been playing blocking canals and sinking ships in my bath?"

Sunday Express, Nov. 18th, 1956

The French and British had attacked Egypt. Ships were sunk by the Egyptians in a blockade of the canal, and the Allied operation was a disaster. The United Nations, which occasionally was able to show its teeth, prevailed, and all military operations by the Anglo-French force came to a halt.

though I nearly bloody well killed myself on one, and I asked Bill – who was going from Hamburg back to Holland – if he would give me a lift. I had kitbags full of stuff which could be strapped into those back satchels on the side. It was amazin' what you could carry on a bike if you were determined enough.

'We set off and just clung on.

'Bill was the kind of rider who would hurtle down

the street straight at a war memorial and just bank round it at the last moment. You were sure you were going to be jam all over the granite, but we always seemed to survive.

'Bill took us through this forest where there were long wide breaks – like avenues – where the trees had been cut down. The trunks had been taken off just six inches from the earth. Bill went straight across the lot of them. Every time we hit a stump I got thrown into the air by about a foot and would then come crashing down on my balls. You could not imagine a less enjoyable manner of leaving behind a world war.'

Giles, who due to his excess booty was told he could not travel back home on a Dakota, took a troop ship from Ostend. Joan was there to meet him.

'I've got you some nice shoes,' Giles told her.

'Oh, where did you get those?' asked Joan.

'I purchased them in a tasteful little shop in ... where was it? I forget, but the nice assistant seemed to think that they would be just the thing.'

CHAPTER SIX

Back Home

Giles returned to Fleet Street a hero. If ever a newspaperman was able to feel secure in his employment, it was he. His war cartoons, for Middle England at any rate, had made him one of the most popular cartoonists ever. And there is no doubt that he did a terrific job raising morale and maintaining it both at home and at the front.

For Lord Beaverbrook, his boss, Giles could do no wrong, and the great man made sure that this feeling was reflected in his pay packet. Lord Beaverbrook's son, Max Aitken, heir to the newspaper group, was soon to take Giles on a casual and mysterious stroll through Hyde Park to the window of Jack Barclay's, the exclusive motor-car showroom in Piccadilly.

'If you wanted one of those which would you choose?' he asked Giles.

Giles pointed to a Bentley Continental. Aitken handed over the keys. That was the heady esteem in which he was now held.

One of his greatest fans and subsequent friends was Michael Bentine, the comedian and fellow 'Goon' along with Peter Sellers, Spike Milligan and Harry Secombe.

'Giles,' explains Bentine, who seems to remember in detail almost every one of Giles's war-time drawings, 'had the ability to reduce all those horrific events to something almost acceptable. Certainly he made everything enormously funny in that English way. But there was something else. Somehow you began to look at reality – things happening about you concerning the war – and then quickly see it as a Giles cartoon.

'There was a marvellous example in 1943 when I was with Bomber Command as an intelligence officer (proving how desperate they really must have been), when one of the Lancaster bombers on the airfield where I was stationed took off and immediately lost two engines. There was nothing that the pilot could do, so he crash-landed. As he did so, in the general panic he pulled up the undercart. The aircraft slewed off to one side on its belly. Well, what the pilot had forgotten was that there was a full bomb load on board. The aircraft started to burn because of all the fuel.

'We ran towards the thing determined to rescue as many as we could. But we then realised that they had escaped. You could see them, funny little figures, running like hell away from the thing – their feet, as it were, two feet above the ground – and they were already on the horizon.

'Someone near said "Cookie". That was the name of the massive bomb they had on board, which soon went off. But as a Giles fan one saw the whole thing as a Giles cartoon. And you could just imagine the

"Someone must have told this son of a sheik we were coming, sergeant."

Sunday Express, Jan. 6th, 1957

A United Nations force was sent in to clear up the mess.

caption under the drawing of the little figures scampering away: "COOKIE".

'There is no doubt that Giles's work had an enormous impact.'

For Giles, back in his studio which he set up in the centre of Ipswich, it was not an entirely easy transition. Suddenly he was without the ready subject matter which had presented itself to him on a daily basis for the past five years. He had lost Hitler and his favourite Musso, and he could no longer draw

"As far as I can make out he wishes to trade you six of his wives and a camel for a carton of Lucky Strike."

Daily Express, May 1st, 1957

cartoons of Tommies and GIs and prattish colonels and Krautish Krauts. Thus it was on 5 August, 1945, just before the Allies dropped the atom bomb on Hiroshima and finally put to an end the war in the Pacific, that Giles introduced The Family. It provided him instantly with a new set of characters, led by Grandma, and they were to dominate his cartoon landscape for the next forty-five years.

Giles had moved permanently to Suffolk, and after a short period in a house on the edge of Ipswich, he moved in October 1946 to Hillbrow Farm. It was there that he and Joan were to stay forever.

Giles, who dispatched his cartoons to the *Express* three times a week by train, became a pig farmer and

man of the land. He dressed very much like a GI, with overalls and an American serviceman's peaked cap, and even drove an American jeep. He built an enormous workshop, transformed the buildings of the farm from dreary to bright, bought himself a racing car and eventually the first of his ocean-going yachts. These were the glittering prizes.

How did he reflect on his war? He is uneasy. As with politics he finds it difficult to express his precise feelings.

'I am anti-war, I suppose,' he says. 'Not pacifist. I think that pacifists have to have more courage than soldiers very often. But on the other hand, I found the war interesting, probably one of the most

"But when the blast of war blows in our ears . . . Stiffen the sinews,
Summon up the blood . . . Clear out the old air-raid shelter . . ."

Sunday Express, April 4th, 1982

On 2 April, 1982, Argentina invaded and captured the Falkland Islands. Britain immediately started assembling a task force. Grandma, Giles's most formidable warrior, is glad to see the end of peace.

"Here she comes—will we take back 200 tins of Argentine corned beef she's been hoarding since Suez?"

Daily Express, April 8th, 1982

interesting times of my life. And I suppose I have to say, like many people, that I enjoyed it. But then how can you say you enjoyed something where there is so much killing?'

Giles, who is sitting now in his wheelchair, a seventy-six-year-old man with a tartan rug round his knees, looks out over his lawn, watching the confounded rabbits attacking his lupins once again, and lapses into silence.

The cartoon of the victory celebrations in the

"At least we know now that the Falkland Islands are not the ones north of the Hebrides and the Orkneys are not somewhere off South America."

Daily Express, April 13th, 1982

summer of 1945, however, was not to be the last time Giles addressed himself to the subject of war. He read in his newspaper on 26 June, 1950: 'Communist North Korea invaded the independent southern half of that troubled country at dawn yesterday. The invasion came without warning. Troops and tanks stormed over the frontier.'

And a day later, the papers reported: 'President

"Out come the old '39–'45 war jokes—'If you want to help our boys you should send those socks to the enemy.'"

Sunday Express, April 25th, 1982

"Off you go and rejoice—and steer clear of the Falklands 200 mile restricted zone."

Daily Express, May 2nd, 1982

"Unconfirmed report that one of your jump-jets has made a direct hit on Dad's cornflakes."

Daily Express, May 4th, 1982

The jump jets of the Falklands War, the Sea Harriers, were the airborne heroes of the hour. Close followers of

Giles will note that Stinker, in the spirit of patriotism, is about to blow up a teddy bear.

Truman ordered American air and naval forces to go to the aid of South Korea.'

It was the beginning of the Korean War, a conflict which soon involved the British and which was to last three years.

Giles found little inspiration for humour in these

"I appreciate the Islanders' wishes are paramount . . . I simply said I wish it wasn't me who makes bloody sure they are."

Daily Express, Jan 20th, 1983

The triumphant British troops settle down in the Falklands for a long stay.

distant hostilities, even though the Tommies were once again involved.

'I think at that time I was actually sympathising with the North Koreans,' he says.

In 1956, the Egyptian President, Colonel Nasser, seized control of the Suez Canal. Despite strong

184

American objections, the British and French sent in troops. The whole operation was a disaster, and the invading forces withdrew ignominiously.

Giles touched on the subject in his weekly drawings for the *Express*, but was disapproving. 'It was a balls-up,' he says. 'I was absolutely against it. We didn't gain anything. By that time, in any case, I had finally become anti any kind of war for whatever reason.

'The Americans had no right to go to Vietnam, and it was a good thing that they were eventually thrown out. If they hadn't gone in the first place tens of thousands of people would now be alive – and I'm sure the map wouldn't have looked any different. The paranoia about Communism was ridiculous.'

The Falklands? Says Giles, who drew a few mainly home-based cartoons of the event: 'I didn't approve of it. Once again it was the British sending in the gunboats.'

And Ulster? 'I hold the soldiers in admiration. I think they are amazin'. But I think we should get out,' says Giles.

It is interesting to hear him all these years later, having enjoyed a life marked by its lack of simple living or austerity, in which he has mingled happily with titled industrialists and royalty as well as with those of the fields and taverns of Suffolk, expressing the kind of view which he first formed in his days at the Communist Sunday journal, *Reynolds News*.

For everything he says is surely what those heroes of his, the journal's principal commentators, Monty Slater and Alan Hutt, would themselves have said at the bar of the Pindar of Wakefield just down the road from King's Cross.

Epilogue

It is spring, 1994. Giles sits by the French windows of Hillbrow Farm as his loving and ever-attentive wife, Joan, prepares lunch. Look about him and you will understand, in part, Giles's life. There is a neat display on the wall of some of his best colour work. There is a bar in the shape of half a clinker-built yacht's hull on which there is a generous array of bottles, a plate of peanuts, and a corkscrew. A shelf holds enough glasses for a large party.

On the windowsills are Dinky toys: little newspaper delivery vans, buses, taxis and lorries. Against the wall stands one of the football games where you twiddle handles to activate the players. On lower shelves there are board games, puzzles and an old draughts set, the cardboard corners worn and the lid ill-fitting with age.

Everywhere there are photographs of yachts and gleaming racing cars and celebrities, including Frank Sinatra and Margot Fonteyn, the latter signed in ink with affectionate and flowing messages. Of 'Giles at War' there is not even a hint.

Does he have anything, now, which touches that distant passage in his life?

'Joan,' he calls. Joan appears, an oven glove on her right hand. 'Yes, Carl?'

'Get that cardboard box for me, will you? The one in the kitchen.'

'There is no cardboard box, Carl. I don't know what you're talking about,' she says.

'It's been there for forty years,' says Carl, shifting with his usual impatience. 'On the top shelf above the sink.'

'I'll have a look,' says Joan, resigned and patient as ever.

'Bloody women,' he says when his incomparably saintly wife has gone to search. 'They never know where anythin' is.'

There is the scraping sound of a step-ladder and a long pause.

Some moments later Joan places a cardboard container, covered with dust and cobwebs, on the table by Giles's wheelchair. 'Is this it?'

Giles pulls it towards him. He takes out a ceremonial dagger in its sheath and a scarlet armband displaying a black swastika.

'These belonged to the commandant of Belsen,' he says. 'They are not mementoes, as such, but they are certainly reminders of the only thing in my life which could not be expressed in a cartoon. Not a day goes by when I do not think of Belsen. I am as haunted and horrified as the day I entered those gates. These objects represent the purest evil you can imagine.'

The grim souvenirs are replaced in the box and pushed away.

"She's here to get Ted Heath."

Sunday Express, Oct. 21st 1990

Former Tory Prime Minister, Ted Heath, had gone to deal with Saddam Hussein about hostages. Grandma has never been too keen on 'deals'.

This brings us to the end of the three volumes on the life and work of this remarkable figure; this difficult, funny, irascible, perceptive, warm, intolerant and, in the end, deeply lovable, compassionate and gentle observer of the latter half of our century.

He made his name in that devastating 1939–1945 conflict, so it seems appropriate to ask him, in conclusion: 'What do you think of war?'

Giles adjusts his position in his wheelchair and puckers his features. He is ill-at-ease when asked to make grand philosophical pronouncements. That has never been his role. After a long pause, during which he adjusts the tartan rug over his knees, he says: 'I hate killin'.'

We fall silent. There is a sizzling from the kitchen and there is the ordered clatter of saucepan lids. Heavenly smells, drawn by the open French windows, drift about our nostrils.

Giles, the uneasy way of the world now forgotten, is ferociously preoccupied with the rabbits at his flowerbed. 'Look at the little sods.

'Joan,' he calls. 'Get my gun.'

War on rabbits. Now that's another story.